WINNIE
~THE~
POOH

The Pooh Dictionary

The Pooh Dictionary

In *The Pooh Dictionary*, the words and phrases that make communication in the Hundred Acre Wood so delightful are gathered together alphabetically. Author A. R. Melrose has meticulously documented the lexicon of Pooh, with the endearingly misused terms, made-up words and childlike phrases which have made A. A. Milne stories such classics of English literature. Equally interesting to the Pooh scholar or the casual reader, this appealing book explores the subtleties – and the humour – of the language of Winnie-the-Pooh.

A. R. Melrose lives in Auckland, New Zealand. He writes full-time and tries to cope with a family over-run by a great many bears. His interests include reading, going to the library and hanging out in second-hand book stores. While he loves Pooh, Eeyore is his most preferred Forest Animal. *The Pooh Dictionary* is Mr Melrose's first book using short words. He holds a university degree in Indian religious thought, but has become a follower of the early Greek philosopher, Epicurus. He also studied for a doctorate within the field of sociology of knowledge, but decided to spend more time having ordinary thoughts.

EGMONT

We bring stories to life

First published in the United States of America 1995 by Dutton Children's Books
First published in Great Britain 1995 by Methuen Children's Books
This edition published 2005 by Egmont Books Limited
239 Kensington High Street, London W8 6SA

Text copyright © 1995 A.R. Melrose
The right of A.R. Melrose to be identified as author of this work has been
asserted by him in accordance with the Copyright, Designs and Patent Act 1988
Text by A. A. Milne and line illustrations by E.H. Shepard from *Winnie-the-Pooh,*
The House at Pooh Corner, When We Were Very Young, Now We Are Six.
Copyright under the Berne Convention.
Grateful acknowledgement is made to the Trustees of the Pooh Properties for use
of the quoted material by A.A. Milne and line illustrations by E.H. Shepard

A CIP catalogue record for this title is available from The British Library

ISBN 1 4052 2169 0
1 3 5 7 9 10 8 6 4 2
Printed in Italy

WINNIE ~THE~ POOH

The Pooh Dictionary

The Complete Guide
to The Words of Pooh and All
The Animals in The Forest

A. R. MELROSE

From the Stories by A. A. Milne
With Decorations by Ernest H. Shepard

EGMONT

CONTENTS

CONTRIBUTION

(or How This Book Came to Be Written)

Pooh, Piglet, and I were lying in that part of the Forest that was nice for picnics, and we were watching the clouds go by slowly. Well, Pooh and Piglet were watching the clouds, and I was trying to read and not doze off.

'Yes,' said Pooh suddenly. 'There is nothing better . . .'

'Yes,' said Piglet in total agreement.

And they both lay in silence again.

'Pardon me,' I said, putting down my book.

Piglet jumped up and began dusting himself down. 'Why? Are you leaving so soon?' he asked.

'No, no, I mean, what did you just mean?' I said.

Pooh sat up and looked at me carefully, and then at Piglet just as carefully.

'Piglet,' he said, 'what did you say? I didn't hear.'

But Piglet said he hadn't said anything, except

1

to be polite, and that I was the one who had said something about leaving, and then meaning something else.

'Just as I thought,' said Pooh very kindly toward me. 'Too much Education and Learning from Books,' he said. 'Rabbit and Owl are almost the same – too many words and not enough – well, never mind,' he said. 'We can't all be Bears – and Piglets of course, Piglet.'

I tried to explain that what *I* meant was that I didn't quite understand what he meant by 'there is nothing better' and what Piglet meant by saying 'yes,' but Piglet said he knew exactly what Pooh said, and Pooh agreed he said exactly what he knew.

'Look,' I said.

'Where?' said Piglet, starting to get a little nervous.

'No, I meant – oh, bothersome Bear and bothersome Piglet!' And then seeing how crestfallen they both had become, I apologized and tried to explain that sometimes I just didn't understand them at all, and it was all my fault, and Pooh said, 'There, there,' and Piglet tried not to snivel, and finally Tigger and Roo turned up, asking us if we thought it was a wonderful day, and then Eeyore joined us, complaining that he just knew everyone would have a picnic and forget to invite him.

'And some might say, *not* forget him,' he said, 'if you know what I mean.'

To cut a long story short, Pooh went on to explain to everyone that I had difficulty with understanding the way they talked. And so Roo went off to get Rabbit and Tigger bounced off to get Owl, because everyone (except me) thought those two knew a lot about words. And when all the Forest Animals had finally gathered around, Eeyore (of all people) suggested that I needed something I could read, since I obviously had some kind of hearing problem, and Owl suggested an Encyclopaedia of sorts.

So we formed a Committee, which pleased Rabbit, and went on to plan the Idea of this Book: The Complete Guide to the Words of Pooh and All the Animals in the Forest. Pooh had wanted to call it an *Almanac*, because Christopher Robin had once shown him one full of complicated tables and lists, but no one had heard of such a thing. Owl suggested *Encyclopaedia*, and everyone just politely ignored him, for it was, after all, rather too long a word. So, Dictionary it is – *The Pooh Dictionary*.

3

ACKNOWLEDGMENTS

(or Thanks To)

Thanks to the friends who indulged me during the writing of this Entertainment: Rosamund Averton, Gwenda Jensen, Debra Penn, John Stuart, and Maggy Woodhams. Helen Fearnley gave the tip to work regularly and often. I am grateful to David Honey, Audrey Griffiths, Liz Morgan, and Karen Naftel for help in coping with the use of the wrong software on the wrong machines (five, to be exact!).

I have very much appreciated the encouragement and collaboration of Joan Powers, Pooh Editor at Dutton Children's Books. I thank also The Trustees of the Pooh Properties.

My wife, Louise Mason, gave me the privilege of having the terrors and joys of raising little Rebecca Janet (and now the baby dynamo, Sally Helena), but also the time for writing and editing this book.

For a book about a Bear and his Friends,

ACKNOWLEDGEMENTS

I cannot but also mention the endless love and pleasure of the two bears in my life – one because he shared a childhood, the other because he has never been absent from a marriage bed of thirteen years. So, to these two I dedicate this book:

Edward (Teddy) Panda

and

Erik T. Bear

IMPORTANT NOTICE

(or How to Use This Book)

Everything in *The Pooh Dictionary* is based upon the texts of *Winnie-the-Pooh* and *The House At Pooh Corner,* specifically the classic colour illustrated editions published in paperback by Egmont Books. All the numbers you find refer to the page numbers of those books.

• All Entries in The Pooh Dictionary are in strict alphabetical order, regardless of Capitals, Hyphens, Apostrophes, or Hesitations:

Friday

Friendly Day

Friend of Piglet

Friends-and-Relations

- All Entries follow the same format:

WORD OR PHRASE BEING DEFINED

PART OF SPEECH

Afternoon, *noun*: **1** a person of Royal Personage but not quite. **2** hence, anyone not nearly as important as you believe or have heard.

DEFINITION: IF THERE IS MORE THAN ONE, THEY ARE NUMBERED

Pooh … said suddenly to Christopher Robin:

'Is it a very Grand thing to be an Afternoon, what you said?'

'A what?' said Christopher Robin lazily, as he listened to something else.

'On a horse,' explained Pooh.

'A Knight?'

'Oh, was that it?' said Pooh.

EXCERPT FROM TEXT OF ORIGINAL BOOKS

(THE HOUSE AT POOH CORNER, page 173)

QUOTE CAN BE FOUND IN THIS BOOK: ON THIS PAGE

See Also: **Sir Pooh De Bear, Knight.**

SEE ALSO: WORDS THAT ARE RELATED IN MEANING OR USE

We use the expression *phrasal* to indicate that within the Entry the phrase we are defining has a meaning independent of the individual meanings of the individual words. For example, **Mysterious Missage** is defined differently from **Missage** and cannot be understood in terms of whatever *mysterious* might mean. Well, perhaps a little bit.

Many Entries ask you to *Refer* to another Entry. This indicates that the Entries mean the same thing or very close to it. *Compare* is used to indicate another Entry that may look or sound as if it is similar in meaning but isn't. We also use an asterisk (*) to highlight any word or phrase that has its own Entry in the *Dictionary*. Like this: **Big Boots***. This saves us from having to reuse *See Also: or Refer.*

We have not provided a guide to the correct pronunciation of the words used in the Forrest. There are several reasons for this, but the principal reason is that words will always sound different if you are Small (and have a squeaky voice) or Large (and have a bellowy voice), or if you just happen to have a mouth full of a Little Something at that moment. We are not convinced that one shouldn't speak with a mouth full of, say, honey (or haycorns).

In general, we have stuck to the way things are spelled in *Winnie-the-Pooh* and *The House At Pooh Corner*, even if they look funny. If there are variations in spelling, we list these under separate entries with cross-referencing. (We find that certain spellings suit certain situations.)

Finally, we should explain our use of dots. We use four dots (. . . .) in Quotes to indicate that some text has been omitted. This has been done with Owl's insistence for literary accuracy. Three dots indicate dots that appear in the original work.

Very Finally, Rabbit wants to point out (that is, thrust his paws excitedly into my face as I type this) that *The Pooh Dictionary* is an Interpretative Guide, which means we spent so long analyzing and fussing over many of the Entries that we still don't feel confident we have got it right. Also, some words got left out. We are not sure which ones, but we have our suspicions.

$\mathcal{A}a$

A, *noun*: **1** the first letter of the Alphabet. We are not sure why this is so. Possibly **A** won some sort of contest with the other letters, or it could very well be that all the other letters are quite shy and **A** isn't. On the other paw, **A** is often called the *indefinite article,* which leads us to believe that **A** has been forced to go first (and so **A** could be very anxious indeed). **2** some authorities (namely Eeyore) understand **A** to mean the same thing as Education, but the connection, surely, is simply because **A** is the first letter in the Alphabet, and *being* **Educated*** means knowing *all* twenty-three or so letters of it.

> 'Do you know what this is?'
> 'No,' said Piglet.
> 'It's an A.'

11

'Oh,' said Piglet.

'Not O, A,' said Eeyore severely. 'Can't you *hear,* or do you think you have more education than Christopher Robin?'

'Yes,' said Piglet. 'No,' said Piglet very quickly . . . .

'Do you know what A means, little Piglet?'

'No, Eeyore, I don't.'

'It means Learning, it means Education, it means all the things that you and Pooh haven't got. That's what A means.'

'Oh,' said Piglet again. 'I mean, does it?' he explained quickly.

. . . . 'That, for instance,' (went on Eeyore,) 'is –'

'An A,' said Rabbit, 'but not a very good one . . . .'

Eeyore looked at his sticks and then he looked at Piglet.

'What did Rabbit say it was?' he asked.

'An A,' said Piglet.

'Did you tell him?'

'No, Eeyore, I didn't. I expect he just knew.'

'He *knew*? You mean this A thing is a thing

Rabbit knew?'

'Yes, Eeyore. He's clever, Rabbit is.'

'Clever!' said Eeyore scornfully, putting a foot heavily on his three sticks. 'Education!' said Eeyore bitterly, jumping on his six sticks. 'What *is* Learning?' asked Eeyore as he kicked his twelve sticks into the air. 'A thing *Rabbit* knows! Ha!'

'I think –' began Piglet nervously.

'Don't,' said Eeyore.

'I think *Violets* are rather nice,' said Piglet.

(THE HOUSE AT POOH CORNER, pages 84–87)

Accident, *noun*: **1** any event that unexpectedly happens so as to cause you to feel not totally quite on top of things. **2** a form of watery transportation in which you are underneath *it* (whereas if *it* is underneath *you*, then it is called a boat).

And Eeyore whispered back: 'I'm not saying there won't be an Accident *now*, mind you. They're funny things, Accidents. You never have them till you're having them.'

(THE HOUSE AT POOH CORNER, page 67)

'Now then, Pooh,' said Christopher Robin, 'where's your boat?'

'I ought to say,' explained Pooh as they walked down to the shore of the island, 'that it isn't just an ordinary sort of boat. Sometimes it's a Boat, and sometimes it's more of an Accident. It all depends.'

'Depends on what?'

'On whether I'm on the top of it or underneath it.'

(**WINNIE-THE-POOH**, pages 128–129)

See Also: **Boat; Floating Bear; Umbrella;** *and* **Very Bad Accident**.

Adventure, *noun*: Any event or happening that requires Fortitude and Footwear. Smaller Animals may require **Provisions*** and, certainly, a **Smackerel*** or two.

Christopher Robin was sitting outside his door, putting on his Big Boots. As soon as he saw the Big Boots, Pooh knew that an Adventure was going to happen, and he brushed the honey off his nose with the back of his paw, and spruced himself up as well as he could, so as to look Ready for Anything.

(**WINNIE-THE-POOH**, page 100)

See Also: **Expedition; Expotition; Hunt;** *and* **North Pole.**

Affectionate Disposition, *phrasal noun*:

An animal is said to have such a disposition when it either has Young and enjoys the sunshine or lacks Fierceness. However, neither of these definitions holds true for the winter months.

Piglet was so excited at the idea of being Useful that he forgot to be frightened any more, and when Rabbit went on to say that Kangas were only Fierce during the winter months, being at other times of an Affectionate Disposition, he could hardly sit still, he was so eager to begin being useful at once.

(**WINNIE-THE-POOH**, page 85)

See Also: **Company; Fierce Animal; Fiercer Animal, Deprived Of Its Young;** *and* **Friendly Day.**

Afternoon, *noun*: **1** a person of Royal Personage but not quite. **2** hence, anyone not nearly as important as you believe or have heard.

Pooh . . . . said suddenly to Christopher Robin:

'Is it a very Grand thing to be an Afternoon, what you said?'

'A what?' said Christopher Robin lazily, as he listened to something else.

'On a horse,' explained Pooh.

'A Knight?'

'Oh, was that it?' said Pooh.

(**THE HOUSE AT POOH CORNER**, page 173)

See Also: **Sir Pooh De Bear, Knight.**

Afterwards, *noun*: That exact moment immediately following an awful, if not deeply frightening, moment when some animal suddenly realizes you have done a thing to really annoy it. It comes directly before that moment when you wish you had had a **Long Start*** or even that **Rescue Is Coming***.

PLAN TO CAPTURE BABY ROO

. . . . I could run away with Roo . . . . Quickly . . . . *And Kanga wouldn't discover the difference until Afterwards.*

Well, Rabbit read this out proudly, and for a little while after he had read it nobody said anything. And then Piglet, who had been opening and shutting his mouth without making any noise, managed to say very huskily:

'And – Afterwards?'

(WINNIE-THE-POOH, pages 85–87)

Aha!, *exclamation* or *interjection*: **1** very specifically, 'We'll tell you where Baby Roo is, if you promise to go away from the Forest and never come back.' **2** generally, however, it means 'I'm not as foolish as I look, and I know what is going on, or at least I think I do.'

'The best way,' said Rabbit, 'would be this. The best way would be to steal Baby Roo and hide him, and then when Kanga says, "Where's Baby Roo?" we say, "*Aha!*"'

'*Aha!*' said Pooh, practising. '*Aha! Aha!* . . . Of course,' he went on, 'we could say "*Aha!*" even if we hadn't stolen Baby Roo.'

'Pooh,' said Rabbit kindly, 'you haven't any brain.'

'I know,' said Pooh humbly.

'We say "*Aha!*" so that Kanga knows that we know where Baby Roo is. "*Aha!*" means "We'll tell you where Baby Roo is, if you promise to go away from the Forest and never come back." Now don't talk while I think.'

(WINNIE-THE-POOH, pages 83–84)

Ambush, *noun*: A type of plant; in fact, a range of quite Fierce Plants, including gorse-bushes, that leap out at you suddenly.

Christopher Robin saw at once how dangerous it was.

'It's just the place,' he explained, 'for an Ambush.'

'What sort of bush?' whispered Pooh to Piglet. 'A gorse-bush?'

'My dear Pooh,' said Owl in his superior way, 'don't you know what an Ambush is? . . . . An Ambush,' said Owl, 'is a sort of Surprise.'

'So is a gorse-bush sometimes,' said Pooh . . . . 'If people jump out at you suddenly, that's an Ambush,' said Owl . . . .

Pooh, who now knew what an Ambush was, said that a gorse-bush had sprung at him suddenly one day when he fell off a tree, and he

had taken six days to get all the prickles out of himself.

'We are not *talking* about gorse-bushes,' said Owl a little crossly.

'I am,' said Pooh.

(WINNIE-THE-POOH, pages 107–08)

Anxiety, *noun*: A condition that arises when, instead of a gorse-bush leaping out at you, a Heffalump leaps out at you, which is usually not pleasant at all. Unfortunately, Small Animals who are of an **Anxious*** Disposition are frequently prone to Heffalump Surprises.

It was not long before [Christopher Robin] came to the Gravel Pit, and he looked down, and there were Pooh and Piglet, with their backs to him, dreaming happily.

'Ho-*ho*!' said Christopher Robin loudly and suddenly.

Piglet jumped six inches in the air with Surprise and Anxiety, but Pooh went on dreaming.

'It's the Heffalump!' thought Piglet nervously.

(THE HOUSE AT POOH CORNER, page 47)

Anxious, *adjective*: You can be said to be in this state when you feel rather lonely, especially if you are only a Very Small Animal and can't do anything except wish you were Not So Small and were able to **Fly*** or jump or make Help-Noises.

It rained and it rained and it rained . . . .

The little dry ditches in which Piglet had nosed about so often had become streams, the little streams across which he had splashed were rivers, and the river, between whose steep banks they had played so happily, had sprawled out of its own bed and was taking up so much room everywhere, that Piglet was beginning to wonder whether it would be coming into *his* bed soon.

'It's a little Anxious,' he said to himself, 'to be a Very Small Animal Entirely Surrounded by Water. Christopher Robin and Pooh could escape by Climbing Trees, and Kanga could escape by Jumping, and Rabbit could escape by Burrowing, and Owl could escape by Flying, and Eeyore could escape by – by Making a Loud Noise Until Rescued, and here am I, surrounded by water and I can't do *anything*.'

(**WINNIE-THE-POOH, pages 117–18**)

See Also: **Anxiety; Blinch;** *and* **Pluck.**

Astute, *adjective*: A term of admiration used toward any Friendly Animal who is noticeably Plumpish.

An idea came to him.

'Owl,' said Pooh, 'I have thought of something.'

'Astute and Helpful Bear,' said Owl.

Pooh looked proud at being called a stout and helpful bear, and said modestly that he just happened to think of it.

(**THE HOUSE AT POOH CORNER, page 138**)

Awful Mistake, *phrasal noun*: **1** quite specifically, the relocation of Eeyore's house without his knowledge or permission. **2** hence, any well-intentioned act that involves the possible loss of everything a person owns, cherishes, or honours.

See Also: **Grand Idea;** *and* **Noble Thing.**

Bb

B, *noun*: What Bears have on their pencils to show not only ownership but what sort of Bear they are. For example, a pencil is marked **B** to show it belongs to a Bear, but **BB** to show it belongs to a Brave Bear. So, a **3B** is owned by a Doubly Brave Bear. Quite Technical.

> When Pooh saw what it was, he nearly fell down, he was so pleased. It was a Special Pencil Case. There were pencils in it marked 'B' for Bear, and pencils marked 'HB' for Helping Bear, and pencils marked 'BB' for Brave Bear.

> **(WINNIE-THE-POOH, page 144)**

See Also: **Special Pencil Case.**

Backson, *noun*: A shy and retiring animal to most but Friendly to some, this animal is always busy, mostly in the morning, and is either Spotted or, at the very least, Herbaceous.

'Ha!' said Rabbit, feeling quite happy again. 'Another notice!'

This is what it said:

GON OUT
BACKSON
BISY
BACKSON.
C. R.

. . . . 'Amazing,' said Owl, looking at the notice again, and getting, just for a moment, a curious sort of feeling that something had happened to Christopher Robin's back . . . .

25

Owl looked at the notice again. To one of his education the reading of it was easy . . .

'It is quite clear what has happened, my dear Rabbit,' he said. 'Christopher Robin has gone out somewhere with Backson. He and Backson are busy together. Have you seen a Backson anywhere about in the Forest lately?'

'I don't know,' said Rabbit. 'That's what I came to ask you. What are they like?'

'Well,' said Owl, 'the Spotted or Herbaceous Backson is just a –'

'At least,' he said, 'it's really more of a –'

'Of course,' he said, 'it depends on the –'

(THE HOUSE AT POOH CORNER, pages 74–78)

Balloon, *noun*: **1** a Big Colored Thing, Full of Puff, that triggers in Animals (Larger and Smaller) a sense of hilarity, song, and the muddling movement of feet, paws, or hooves. **2** a Big Colored Thing, Full of Puff, that you use to **Fly*,** excepting Owls who use wings. Wings or balloons are not recommended for Smaller Animals.

'All right, then,' [said Piglet,] 'I'll give him a balloon. I've got one left from my party. I'll go and get it now, shall I?'

'That, Piglet, is a *very* good idea. It is just what Eeyore wants to cheer him up. Nobody can be uncheered with a balloon.'

. . . . 'Balloon?' said Eeyore. 'You did say balloon? One of those big coloured things you blow up? Gaiety, song-and-dance, here we are and there we are?"

(WINNIE-THE-POOH, pages 71–78)

When the balloon was blown up as big as big, and you and Pooh were both holding on to the string, you let go suddenly, and Pooh Bear floated gracefully up into the sky, and stayed there – level with the top of the tree and about twenty feet away from it.

'Hooray!' you shouted.

(WINNIE-THE-POOH, page 12)

See Also: **Uncheer.**

Bath, *noun*: A process requiring water and soap and flannels and the furious rubbing of your body to remove your comfortable worn-in color. This isn't at all as pleasant as it may sound.

Before he knew where he was, Piglet was in the bath, and Kanga was scrubbing him firmly with a large lathery flannel.

'Ow!' cried Piglet. 'Let me out! I'm Piglet!'

'Don't open your mouth, dear, or the soap goes in,' said Kanga. 'There! What did I tell you?'

'You – you – you did it on purpose,'

spluttered Piglet, as soon as he could speak again . . . . and then accidentally had another mouthful of lathery flannel.

'That's right, dear, don't say anything,' said Kanga, and in another minute Piglet was out of the bath, and being rubbed dry with a towel . . . .

Christopher Robin looked at him very carefully, and shook his head . . . .

'Oh, you're not Piglet,' he said. 'I know Piglet well, and he's *quite* a different colour.'

(**WINNIE-THE-POOH, pages 95–97**)

See Also: **Washing Nonsense (Behind the Ears).**

Bear, Best in All the World, *personal descriptive noun*: Refers to Pooh, and means much the same as 'Bear of No Brain at All,' except perhaps less Foolish and Deluded.

See Also: **No Brain.**

Bear, Eating Habits Thereof, *informational tidbit (that probably shouldn't be in a Dictionary anyway, but we think it's important)*: Regularly and more often than not, especially **Hunny***. **Condensed Milk*** will do, as such food builds an **Enormous Brain***, making you very **Astute***. *Refer:* **Food.**

Bear of No Brain at All, *Refer:* **No Brain.**

Bear with a Positively Startling Lack of Brain, *Refer:* **Positively Startling Lack of Brain.**

Bee, *noun*: A small creature (of the genus *Apis*), notable for buzzing and making **Hunny***.

Belongs, *verb*: Used to mean that you are quite attached to parts of yourself, or that parts of yourself are quite attached to you – if you see the difference.

Eeyore was sitting with his tail in the water . . . .
    'As I expected,' he said. 'Lost all feeling. Numbed it. Well, as long as nobody minds, I suppose it's all right.'
    'Poor old Eeyore! I'll dry it for you,' said Christopher Robin, and he took out his handkerchief and rubbed it up.

'Thank you, Christopher Robin. You're the only one who seems to understand about tails. They don't think – that's what's the matter with some of these others. They've no imagination. A tail isn't a tail to *them*, it's just a Little Bit Extra at the back.'

'Never mind, Eeyore,' said Christopher Robin, rubbing his hardest. 'Is *that* better?'

'It's feeling more like a tail perhaps. It Belongs again, if you know what I mean.'

(**WINNIE-THE-POOH, pages 113–15**)

See Also: **Little Bit Extra.**

Best Thing, *noun*: That which is most aesthetically and emotionally, if not gastronomically, pleasing (so much so you can't really find the right words to describe how wonderfully pleasing it all really is).

Christopher Robin said: 'What do you like doing best in the world, Pooh?'

'Well,' said Pooh, 'what I like best –' and then he had to stop and think. Because although. Eating Honey *was* a very good thing to do, there was a moment just before you began to eat it which was better than when you were, but he didn't know what it was called. And then he thought that being with Christopher Robin was a

very good thing to do, and having Piglet near was a very friendly thing to have; and so, when he had thought it all out, he said, 'What I like best in the whole world is Me and Piglet going to see You, and You saying, "What about a little something?" and Me saying, "Well, I shouldn't mind a little something, should you, Piglet," and it being a hummy sort of day outside, and birds singing.'

(THE HOUSE AT POOH CORNER, pages 168–69)

See Also: **Nothing; Thingish;** *and* **Very Little Brain.**

Big Boots, *phrasal noun*: **1** the Footwear necessary for Enterprise and Excitement. **2** any article of clothing that is only worn when things begin to get quite exciting.

> Christopher Robin was sitting outside his door, putting on his Big Boots. As soon as he saw the Big Boots, Pooh knew that an Adventure was going to happen, and he brushed the honey off his nose with the back of his paw, and spruced himself up as well as he could, so as to look Ready for Anything.
>
> (**WINNIE-THE-POOH, page 100**)

See Also: **Adventure;** *and* **Braces.**

Biscuit Cough, *phrasal noun*: That slight bodily or medical problem that you never mention because everyone else makes such a big fuss of the whole thing, especially when you just want to get on with things.

> 'I don't think Roo had better come,' Rabbit said. 'Not today.'
> 'Why not?' said Roo, who wasn't supposed to be listening.
> 'Nasty cold day,' said Rabbit, shaking his head. 'And you were coughing this morning.'

'How do you know?' asked Roo indignantly.

'Oh, Roo, you never told me,' said Kanga reproachfully.

'It was a Biscuit Cough,' said Roo, 'not one you tell about.'

(THE HOUSE AT POOH CORNER, page 112)

Blinch, *verb*: To hesitate, quaver and quiver, or generally show a little bit of nervousness. Not to blinch is to go as boldly as any Very Small Animal can, which isn't much but is usually enough.

> *O gallant Piglet (PIGLET)! Ho!*
>   *Did Piglet tremble? Did he blinch?*
>   *No, No, he struggled inch by inch*
> *Through LETTERS ONLY, as I know*
> *Because I saw him go.*

(THE HOUSE AT POOH CORNER, page 146)

See Also: **Pluck;** *and* **Ready for Anything.**

Blot, *signature* (at least the attempt at one): Tigger's bold and bouncy name when it is mixed with ink and paper.

'The rissolution,' said Rabbit, 'is that we all sign it, and take it to Christopher Robin.'

So it was signed POOH, PIGLIT, WOL . . . . BLOT.

(THE HOUSE AT POOH CORNER, pages 164–65)

Blusterous, *adjective*: A word used to describe those Atmospheric Conditions in which one's ears are adversely affected (and possibly one's house).

The wind was against them now, and Piglet's ears streamed behind him like banners as he fought his way along, and it seemed hours before he got them into the shelter of the Hundred Acre Wood and they stood up straight again, to listen, a little nervously, to the roaring of the gale among the tree-tops.

.... In a little while [Piglet and Pooh] were knocking and ringing very cheerfully at Owl's door ....

'Correct me if I am wrong,' [Owl] said, 'but am I right in supposing that it is a very Blusterous day outside?'

'Very,' said Piglet, who was quietly thawing his ears, and wishing that he was safely back in his own house.

(**THE HOUSE AT POOH CORNER, pages 129–30**)

See Also: **Belongs;** *and* **Little Bit Extra.**

Boat, *noun*: Something you do things on, particularly if you are wanting to go somewhere, whether wet or dry.

'We're all going on an Expotition with Christopher Robin!'

'What is it when we're on it?'

'A sort of boat, I think,' said Pooh.

'Oh! that sort.'

(**WINNIE-THE-POOH, pages 102–3**)

See Also: **Accident; Escape; Expotition; Floating Bear;** *and* **Umbrella.**

Boff, *verb:* To cough in that very excitable sort of way that Bouncing Sort of Animals, like Tiggers, do quite a lot.

'He just *is* bouncy,' said Piglet, 'and he can't help it.'

. . . . 'All I did was I coughed,' said Tigger.

'He bounced,' said Eeyore.

'Well, I sort of boffed,' said Tigger.

(**THE HOUSE AT POOH CORNER, pages 102–03**)

See Also: **Bounce;** *and* **Coffy.**

Bon-hommy, *foreign noun:* French word for a type of mulberry bush just like an **Ambush***, except not at all Fierce, nor does it exactly leap out at you suddenly. But it can be just as intolerable.

35

'Good morning, Pooh Bear,' said Eeyore gloomily. 'If it *is* a good morning,' he said. 'Which I doubt,' said he.

'Why, what's the matter?'

'Nothing, Pooh Bear, nothing. We can't all, and some of us don't. That's all there is to it.'

'Can't all *what*?' said Pooh, rubbing his nose.

'Gaiety. Song-and-dance. Here we go round the mulberry bush.'

'Oh!' said Pooh. He thought for a long time, and then asked, 'What mulberry bush is that?'

'Bon-hommy,' went on Eeyore gloomily. 'French word meaning bonhommy,' he explained. 'I'm not complaining, but There It Is.'

(**WINNIE-THE-POOH, pages 65–67**)

Bother!, *exclamation*: An exclamatory remark you make when you discover the honey jars are empty and so is your tummy, especially just after a meal. Similarly, you use it whenever your Bodily Constitution is inconvenienced by **Accidents*** or Circumstances. It is the strongest possible exclamatory remark a Very **Small** Animal should make.

'Lucky I brought this with me,' he thought. 'Many a bear going out on a warm day like this would never have thought of bringing a little something with him.' And he began to eat.

36

'Now let me see,' he thought, as he took his last lick of the inside of the jar, 'where was I going? Ah, yes, Eeyore.' He got up slowly.

And then, suddenly, he remembered. He had eaten Eeyore's birthday present!

'*Bother!*' said Pooh.

(WINNIE-THE-POOH, page 72)

'That's me again,' thought Pooh. 'I've had an Accident, and fallen down a well, and my voice has gone all squeaky and works before I'm ready for it, because I've done something to myself inside. Bother!'

(THE HOUSE AT POOH CORNER, pages 38–39)

See Also: **Bothering;** *and (just to see what you shouldn't say)* **Hush!**

Bothering, *adjective*: A description of any other Animal (Smaller or Larger), Thing, or Activity that for whatever reason causes you to exclaim, as Loudly as your Size allows, 'Bother!'

'And it's no good looking at the Six Pine Trees for Piglet,' said Pooh to himself, 'because he's been organdized in a special place of his own. So I shall have to look for the Special Place first. I wonder where it is.' And he wrote it down in his head . . . .

'Which makes it look like a bothering sort of day,' thought Pooh, as he stumped along.

The next moment the day became very bothering indeed, because Pooh was so busy not looking where he was going that he stepped on a piece of the Forest which had been left out by mistake; and he only just had time to think to himself: 'I'm flying. What Owl does. I wonder how you stop – when he stopped.

Bump!

(**THE HOUSE AT POOH CORNER, page 38**)

See Also: **Bother!;** *and* **Fly.**

Bounce, *noun*: **1** what you are full of when you are jolly, exuberant, and Tiggerish; *verb (indicative)*: **2** to be jolly, exuberant, and Tiggerish (especially if you are Tigger and other animals are a little put off); *verb (passive)*: **3** to be surprised when someone is jolly and exuberant when you were not looking. This can lead to an **Accident***.

'How did you fall in, Eeyore?' asked Rabbit, as he dried him with Piglet's handkerchief.

'I didn't,' said Eeyore.

'But how –'

'I was BOUNCED,' said Eeyore.

'Oo,' said Roo excitedly, 'did someone push you?'

'Somebody BOUNCED me. I was just thinking by the side of the river – thinking, if any of you know what that means, when I received a loud BOUNCE.'

'Oh, Eeyore!' said everybody.

'Are you sure you didn't slip?' asked Rabbit wisely.

'Of course I slipped. If you're standing on the slippery bank of a river, and somebody BOUNCES you loudly from behind, you slip. What did you think I did?'

'But who did it?' asked Roo.

Eeyore didn't answer.

'I expect it was Tigger,' said Piglet nervously.

(THE HOUSE AT POOH CORNER, pages 99–100)

Pooh said, 'Let's go and see Kanga and Roo and Tigger,' and Piglet said, 'Y-yes. L-let's' – because he was still a little anxious about Tigger, who was a Very Bouncy Animal, with a way of saying How-do-you-do, which always left your ears full of sand, even after Kanga had said, 'Gently, Tigger dear,' and had helped you up again.

(**THE HOUSE AT POOH CORNER, page 58**)

See Also: **Accident; Boff; Bothering; Coffy;** *and* **Hearty Joke.**

Braces, *noun*: **1** sort of straps slung over your shoulders that, being attached to your trousers, keep them from falling down. **2** paradoxically, any sort of clothing that you find so exciting *you* want to fall down.

> Piglet wasn't listening, he was so agog at the thought of seeing Christopher Robin's blue braces again. He had only seen them once before, when he was much younger, and, being a little over-excited by them, had had to go to bed half an hour earlier than usual; and he had always wondered since if they were really as blue and as bracing as he had thought them.

(**THE HOUSE AT POOH CORNER, page 67**)

Brain, *noun*: That part of the Body that you use to think. There is a connection between the amount of Brain you have and your ability to Think. But this doesn't account for those animals who only have **Fluff*,** or **No Brain*** (or even No Fluff), but can be quite **Clever*** about the most important things in the Forest, like doing the Right Thing to Do, or more importantly, the Next Thing.

> 'There's Pooh,' [Piglet] thought to himself. 'Pooh hasn't much Brain, but he never comes to any harm. He does silly things and they turn out right. There's Owl. Owl hasn't exactly got Brain, but he Knows Things . . . . There's Rabbit. He hasn't Learnt in Books, but he can always Think of a Clever Plan. There's Kanga. She isn't Clever, Kanga isn't, but she would be so anxious about Roo that she would do a Good Thing to Do without thinking about it.'
>
> **(WINNIE-THE-POOH, page 118)**

> 'Owl,' said Rabbit shortly, 'you and I have brains. The others have fluff. If there is any thinking to be done in this Forest – and when I say thinking I mean *thinking* – you and I must do it.'
>
> 'Yes,' said Owl. 'I was.'
>
> **(THE HOUSE AT POOH CORNER, page 76)**

41

[Eeyore said,] 'And I said to myself: the others will be sorry if I'm getting myself all cold. They haven't got Brains, any of them, only grey fluff that's blown into their heads by mistake, and they don't Think.'

(THE HOUSE AT POOH CORNER, page 10)

See Also: **A; Educated; Enormous Brain; Good Thing; Learn in Books; Positively Startling Lack of Brain; Real Brain;** *and* **Very Little Brain.**

Brain, Enormous, *Refer:* Enormous Brain.

Brain, No, *Refer:* No Brain.

Brain of Pooh, *Refer:* Umbrella.

Brain, Positively Startling Lack of, *Refer:* Positively Startling Lack of Brain.

Brain, Real, *Refer:* Real Brain.

Brain, Very Little, *Refer:* Very Little Brain.

Brave and Clever, *phrasal adjective:* Expression of delight in any Small Animal that has a Good Idea, especially an unexpected one.

It wasn't what Christopher Robin expected, and the more he looked at it, the more he thought what a Brave and Clever Bear Pooh was, and the more Christopher Robin thought this, the more Pooh looked modestly down his nose and tried to pretend he wasn't.

(**WINNIE-THE-POOH, page 129**)

Bread, *noun*: A foodstuff easily declined for the sake of Politeness.

[Pooh] was very glad to see Rabbit getting out the plates and mugs; and when Rabbit said, 'Honey or condensed milk with your bread?' he was so excited that he said, 'Both,' and then, so as not to seem greedy, he added, 'but don't bother about the bread, please.' And for a long time after that he said nothing . . . until at last, humming to himself in a rather sticky voice, he got up, shook Rabbit lovingly by the paw, and said that he must be going on.

(WINNIE-THE-POOH, page 23)

See Also: **Bear, Eating Habits Thereof; Breakfast; Condensed Milk; Eleven O'clock; Eleven O'clockish; Hunny; Luncheon Time; Smackerel;** *and* **Tea.**

Breakfast, *noun*: One of the Most Exciting Things About Life.

Pooh and Piglet walked home thoughtfully together in the golden evening, and for a long time they were silent.

'When you wake up in the morning, Pooh,' said Piglet at last, 'what's the first thing you say to yourself?'

'What's for breakfast?' said Pooh. 'What do you say, Piglet?'

'I say, I wonder what's going to happen

exciting *today*?' said Piglet.

Pooh nodded thoughtfully.

'It's the same thing,' he said.

(**WINNIE-THE-POOH, pages 144–45**)

Bump, *noun*: That particular instant when you realize that Life could be simpler, but then you don't have the time to work it out.

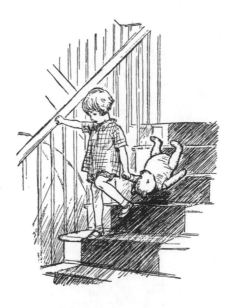

Here is Edward Bear, coming downstairs now, bump, bump, bump, on the back of his head, behind Christopher Robin. It is, as far as he knows, the only way of coming downstairs, but sometimes he feels that there really is another way, if only he could stop bumping for a moment and think of it. And then he feels that perhaps there isn't.

(**WINNIE-THE-POOH, page 1**)

Bumping, *verb*: The art of descending or ascending stairs (depending on whether you are going face first or back-of-the-head first). *Refer:* **Bump.**

Buther, *exclamation*: Poetically, a double **Bother!***, and rarely used in everyday language, which is a good thing, since even **Bother!*** is pretty extreme for some Polite Animals.

(I haven't got a rhyme for that
    'is' in the second line yet.
    Bother.)
(Now I haven't got a rhyme for
    bother. Bother.)
Those two bothers will have
    to rhyme with each other.
    Buther.
        (from POEM, by Eeyore)
(THE HOUSE AT POOH CORNER, pages 162–63)

See Also: **Bothering.**

Cc

Captainish, *adjective*: Describes that indefinable quality of leadership that is grandly impractical, but you don't know in quite what way. You do know, however, that no matter how Captainish a Captain may be, a Captain is a Captain, and you are not.

It was going to be one of Rabbit's busy days. As soon as he woke up he felt important, as if everything depended upon him. It was just the day for Organizing Something, or for Writing a Notice Signed Rabbit, or for Seeing What Everybody Else Thought About It . . . . It was a Captainish sort of day, when everybody said, 'Yes,

Rabbit' and 'No, Rabbit,' and waited until he had told them.

(THE HOUSE AT POOH CORNER, page 71)

See Also: **Organdized, To Be;** *and* **Seeing What Everybody Else Thought About It.**

Capture, *verb*: Steal.

'Never mind, Pooh,' said Piglet impatiently.

'The question is, What are we to do about Kanga?'

'Oh, I see,' said Pooh.

'The best way,' said Rabbit, 'would be this. The best way would be to steal Baby Roo and hide him . . .'

'Now listen all of you,' said Rabbit when he had finished writing, and Pooh and Piglet sat listening very eagerly with their mouths open. This is what Rabbit read out:

PLAN TO CAPTURE BABY ROO
(WINNIE-THE-POOH, pages 83–85)

See Also: **Aha!; Cunning Trap;** *and* **Very Deep Pit.**

Clever, *adjective*: Having the ability to use one's **Brain*** or **Fluff*** in a Surprising and Admirable Way, usually but not always to some purpose. *Refer:* **Clever Idea; Clever Reader;** *and* **Thingish.**

Clever Idea, *phrasal noun*: A thought or notion that surprises even the person who has it, but solves a problem nonetheless.

Of course Pooh would be with him, [Piglet thought,] and it was much more Friendly with two. But suppose Heffalumps were Very Fierce with Pigs *and* Bears? Wouldn't it be better to pretend that he had a headache, and couldn't go up to the Six Pine Trees this morning? But then suppose that it was a very fine day, and there was no Heffalump in the trap, here he would be, in bed all the morning, simply wasting his time for nothing. What should he do?

And then he had a Clever Idea. He would go up very quietly to the Six Pine Trees now, peep very cautiously into the Trap, and see if there *was* a Heffalump there. And if there was, he would go back to bed, and if there wasn't, he wouldn't.

(WINNIE-THE-POOH, page 60–61)

Compare: **Grand Idea.**
See Also: **Very Clever Pup-Pup-Pup Plan.**

Clever Reader, *phrasal noun*: An animal who has sufficient **Brain*** to understand squiggles and dots written in what looks like code.

Pooh plunged into the water, seized the bottle, and struggled back to his tree again.

'Bother!' said Pooh, as he opened it. 'All that wet for nothing. What's that bit of paper doing?'

He took it out and looked at it.

'It's a Missage,' he said to himself, 'that's what it is. And that letter is a 'P,' and so is that, and so is that, and 'P' means 'Pooh,' so it's a very important Missage to me, and I can't read it. I must find Christopher Robin or Owl or Piglet, one of those Clever Readers who can read things, and they will tell me what this message means. Only I can't swim. Bother!'

(WINNIE-THE-POOH, page 123)

See Also: **Spelling.**

Climbing, *noun*: A sport of Fools, Tiggers, and Bears (which shouldn't be surprising).

'Can [Tiggers] climb trees better than Pooh?' asked Roo, stopping under the tallest Pine Tree, and looking up at it.

'Climbing trees is what they do best,' said Tigger. 'Much better than Poohs.'

'Could they climb this one?'

'They're always climbing trees like that,' said Tigger. 'Up and down all day.'

'Oo, Tigger, are they *really*?'

'I'll show you,' said Tigger bravely, 'and you can sit on my back and watch me.' For of all the things which he had said Tiggers could do, the only one he felt really certain about suddenly was climbing trees . . . .

'Hallo, Roo!' called Piglet. 'What are you doing?'

'We can't get down, we can't get down!' cried Roo. 'Isn't it fun? Pooh, isn't it fun, Tigger and I are living in a tree, like Owl, and we're going to stay here for ever and ever . . . . '

'How did you get there, Roo?' asked Piglet.

'On Tigger's back! And Tiggers can't climb downwards, because their tails get in the way, only upwards, and Tigger forgot about that when we started, and he's only just remembered. So we've got to stay here for ever and ever – unless we go higher.'

(THE HOUSE AT POOH CORNER, pages 60, 64)

Cnoke, *verb*: To actively knock with a bell-pull, especially if you don't expect an answer.

Underneath the bell-pull there was a notice which said:

Plez Cnoke if an Rnsr is Not Reqid.
(WINNIE-THE-POOH, page 43)

See Also: **Plez; Reqid; Rnser/Rnsr;** *and* **Spelling.**

Coffy, *adjective*: Describes the jolly, exuberant, and Tiggerish mastications and jaw movements required to clear one's throat and mouth of any insalubrious material, with the effect that a Surprise or an **Accident*** occurs (whether you intended one or not).

'Tigger,' [Rabbit] said solemnly, 'what happened just now?'

'Just when?' said Tigger a little uncomfortably.

'When you bounced Eeyore into the river.'

'I didn't bounce him.'

'You bounced me,' said Eeyore gruffly.

'I didn't really. I had a cough, and I happened to be behind Eeyore . . . . I didn't bounce, I coughed,' said Tiger crossly.

'Bouncy or coffy, it's all the same at the bottom of the river.'

(**THE HOUSE AT POOH CORNER, page 101–02**)

Compare: **Boff.**

Company, *noun:* The situation of not being alone, which can be Quite Pleasant, as it involves a **Little Something (to Revive Oneself)***, and is certainly preferable to having to listen to your own hums and self-doubts. To be recommended to **Anxious*** Small Animals (as well as **Astute*** Animals).

'Rabbit means Company,' [Pooh said to himself,] 'and Company means Food and Listening-to-Me-Humming and such like. *Rum-tum-tum-tiddle-um.'*

(WINNIE-THE-POOH, page 21)

It rained and it rained and it rained . . . .

'If only,' [Piglet] thought, as he looked out of the window, 'I had been in Pooh's house, or Christopher Robin's house, or Rabbit's house when it began to rain, then I should have had Company all this time, instead of being here all alone, with nothing to do except wonder when it will stop.'

(WINNIE-THE-POOH, page 117)

See Also: **Friendly Day.**

Completely Unsettled, *phrasal noun*: That emotional state that usually follows an Incident in which you Completely Misunderstand what is happening and then Completely Become Confused. Similar to **Anxiety***, but without the running away bit. *Refer*: **Unsettle**.

See Also: **Pluck.**

Condensed Milk, *eating tip*: A **Food*** worth keeping in your cupboard for those unexpected moments when a little **Smackerel*** is called for.

Confused Noise, *phrasal noun*: What usually results from the Well-meaning organizing an Event for Everyone Else, especially those who didn't want an Event in the first place.

In a little while they were all ready at the top of the Forest, and the Expotition started . . . .

'What I say,' said Eeyore, 'is that it's

unsettling. I didn't want to come on this Expo – what Pooh said. I only came to oblige. But here I am; and if I am the end of the Expo – what we're talking about – then let me *be* the end. But if, every time I want to sit down for a little rest, I have to brush away half a dozen of Rabbit's smaller friends-and-relations first, then it isn't an Expo – whatever it is – at all, it's simply a Confused Noise. That's what *I* say.'

(**WINNIE-THE-POOH, page 104**)

See Also: **Captainish;** *and* **Organdized, To Be.**

Consideration, *Refer*: **Thought for Others.**

Cottleston Pie, *phrasal noun*: Any nonsense that sounds reasonable.

Cottleston, Cottleston, Cottleston Pie,
Why does a chicken, I don't know why.
Ask me a riddle and I reply:
'*Cottleston, Cottleston, Cottleston Pie.*'

(**WINNIE-THE-POOH, page 68**)

See Also: **Hum.**

Crustimoney Proseedcake, *phrasal noun*: Means the same as 'customary procedure' (which means the Thing to Do), but implies the necessity for eating as well (hence the references to cake, seed, and crust).

'Well,' said Owl, 'the customary procedure in such cases is as follows.'

'What does Crustimoney Proseedcake mean?' said Pooh. 'For I am a Bear of Very Little Brain, and long words Bother me.'

'It means the Thing to Do,' said Owl.

'As long as it means that, I don't mind,' said Pooh humbly.

(WINNIE-THE-POOH, page 45)

Cunning Trap, *phrasal noun*: The way of capturing another animal by Complicated and Chance-Dependent Steps (at least ten). *Refer:* **Very Deep Pit.**

Dd

Disgrace, *noun*: A dwelling place that has become dirty, damp, dank, disgusting, despicable, disgraceful, and lots of other words beginning with *d*.

Every now and then Roo fell in and came back on the rope with the next article, which flustered Kanga a little because she never knew where to look for him. So she got cross with Owl and said that his house was a Disgrace, all damp and dirty, and it was quite time it did tumble down. Look at that horrid bunch of toadstools growing out of the floor there! So Owl looked down, a little surprised because he didn't know about this.

(**THE HOUSE AT POOH CORNER, page 152–53**)

See Also: **Spudge.**

Don't Blame Me, *phrase of intent*: What you should say when you take no responsibility for what might happen despite the fact you are participating in whatever is happening.

'Come on!' called Christopher Robin . . . .

'We're starting,' said Rabbit. 'I must go.' And he hurried off to the front of the Expotition with Christopher Robin.

'All right,' said Eeyore. 'We're going. Only Don't Blame Me.'

So off they all went to discover the North Pole.

(**WINNIE-THE-POOH, page 105**)

See Also: **Confused Noise; Expotition;** *and* **Seeing What Everybody Else Thought About It.**

Ee

Early, *Refer:* **Late and Early.**

East Pole, *phrasal noun*: A place that doesn't exist and isn't even pleasant to dream about.

> Then suddenly [Pooh] was dreaming. He was at the East Pole, and it was a very cold pole with the coldest sort of snow and ice all over it. He had found a bee-hive to sleep in, but there wasn't room for his legs, so he had left them outside. And Wild Woozles, such as inhabit the East Pole, came and nibbled all the fur off his legs to make nests for their Young. And the more they nibbled, the colder his legs got, until suddenly he woke up with an *Ow!*
>
> **(WINNIE-THE-POOH, page 122)**

See Also: **North Pole;** *and* **Poles (Other).**

E.C. and T.F., *abbreviations:* **Eeyore's Comforter and Tail-finder*.** *Refer:* **Winnie-The-Pooh, Honorific Titles Thereof.**

Educated, *adjective:* Having Education. *Refer:* **A.**

Education, *Refer:* **A.**

Edward Bear, *proper name:* Real name of Winnie-the-Pooh.

Ee-ers O I A-ors, *phrasal noun:* **1** specifically, what Tiggers say when they have a mouth full of acorns and wish to convey the thought that spitting food should not be considered an impolite thing to do. **2** *phrasal adjective:* describes any food, especially expensive, that tastes like chewed haycorns.

> '[Tiggers] like haycorns,' said Pooh, 'so that's what we've come for, because poor Tigger hasn't had any breakfast yet.'
> Piglet pushed the bowl of haycorns towards Tigger, and said: 'Help yourself,' and then he got close up to Pooh and felt much braver, and said, 'So you're Tigger? Well, well!' in a careless sort of voice. But Tigger said nothing because his mouth was full of haycorns . . . .

After a long munching noise he said:

'Ee-ers o i a-ors.'

And when Pooh and Piglet said 'What?' he said 'Skoos ee,' and went outside for a moment.

When he came back he said firmly:

'Tiggers don't like haycorns.'

'But you said they liked everything except honey,' said Pooh.

'Everything except honey *and* haycorns,' explained Tigger.

(**THE HOUSE AT POOH CORNER, pages 23–24**)

See Also: **Food.**

Eeyore's Comforter and Tail-finder,
Refer: **Winnie-The-Pooh, Honorific Titles Thereof.**

Eleven O'clock, *phrasal noun*: That time (usually Late Morning) about which a Bear (or Smaller Animal) likes (and needs) a **Little Something (to Revive One-self)***.

Pooh always liked a little something at eleven o'clock in the morning, and he was very glad to see Rabbit getting out the plates and mugs.

(**WINNIE-THE-POOH, page 23**)

When [Pooh] suddenly saw Piglet sitting in his best arm-chair, he could only stand there rubbing his head and wondering whose house he was in.

'Hallo, Piglet,' he said. 'I thought you were out.'

'No,' said Piglet, 'it's you who were out, Pooh.'

'So it was,' said Pooh. 'I knew one of us was.'

He looked at his clock, which had stopped at five minutes to eleven some weeks ago.

'Nearly eleven o'clock,' said Pooh happily. 'You're just in time for a little smackerel of something,' and he put his head into the cupboard. 'And then we'll go out, Piglet . . . .'

The clock was still saying five minutes to eleven when Pooh and Piglet set out on their way half an hour later.

(THE HOUSE AT POOH CORNER, pages 2–4)

Compare: **Breakfast;** *and* **Luncheon Time.**
See Also: **Eleven O'Clockish; Funny Feeling;** *and* **Smackerel.**

Eleven O'clockish, *phrasal noun*: That bodily sensation, which is similar to a **Funny Feeling*,** occurring in the Late Morning, that lets you know it *is* **Eleven O'clock*,** or very close to it.

Kanga said very kindly, 'Well, look in my cupboard, Tigger dear, and see what you'd like.' . . . .

'Shall I look, too?' said Pooh, who was beginning to feel a little eleven o'clockish. And he found a small tin of condensed milk . . . . so he took it into a corner by itself and went with it to see that nobody interrupted it.

(THE HOUSE AT POOH CORNER, pages 30–31)

Encyclopaedia, *a very long noun:* Refer: **Interesting Anecdote.**

Enormous Brain, *phrasal noun:* Generally, any animal who eats a lot (that is, as often as possible and in pleasant **Company***) is said to be 'of Enormous Brain.' The word *Brain* does not in this context refer to the space or **Fluff*** between the ears, but is a word that stands for the Astuter Parts of One's Anatomy, especially the stomach.

I am talking of Pooh –
(*Of who?*)
Of Pooh!
(*I'm sorry I keep forgetting.*)
Well, Pooh was a Bear of Enormous Brain
(*Just say it again!*)
Of enormous brain –
(*Of enormous what?*)
Well, he ate a lot.

(WINNIE-THE-POOH, page 136)

See Also: **Astute;** *and* **Bear, Eating Habits Thereof.**

Eor, *nom de plume*: **Eeyore.**

'The rissolution,' said Rabbit, 'is that we all sign it, and take it to Christopher Robin.'

So it was signed POOH, PIGLIT, WOL, EOR . . . .
(**THE HOUSE AT POOH CORNER, page 164**)

Escape, *verb*: **1** to get away from and avoid (usually as quickly as possible); *noun*: **2** the method or vehicle one uses to *get away from* (very quickly).

When the rain began Pooh was asleep. It rained, and it rained, and it rained, and he slept and he slept and he slept. He had had a tiring day . . . . Suddenly he woke up with an *Ow!*

– and there he was, sitting in his chair with his feet in the water, and water all round him!

He splashed to his door and looked out . . . .

'This is Serious,' said Pooh. 'I must have an Escape.'

So he took his largest pot of honey and escaped with it to a broad branch of his tree, well above the water, and then he climbed down again and escaped with another pot ... and when the whole Escape was finished, there was Pooh sitting on his branch, dangling his legs, and there, beside him, were ten pots of honey.

(WINNIE-THE-POOH, pages 121–22)

'I think it was the wind,' said Piglet. 'I think your house has blown down.' . . . .

Owl coughed in an unadmiring sort of way,

and said that, if Pooh was sure that *was* all, they could now give their minds to the Problem of Escape.

'Because,' said Owl, 'we can't go out by what used to be the front door. Something's fallen on it.'

'But how else *can* you go out?' asked Piglet anxiously.

'That is the Problem, Piglet, to which I am asking Pooh to give his mind.'

(**THE HOUSE AT POOH CORNER,
pages 135–37**)

See Also: **Serious.**

Etceteras, *plural noun*: The exact way to use this form of address correctly is uncertain. It can be used when you are trying to indicate to an indifferent Poetry audience that if they are not **What-nots***, they are pretty close to it as Etceteras. The literary nature of the word is shown by the use of *Etceteras* at the end of long sentences (or short ones) in Deep and Meaningful Books or Notices and seems to be quite an acceptable way of addressing your unknown readers.

[Eeyore] coughed in an important way, and began again: 'What-nots and Etceteras, before I

begin, or perhaps I should say, before I end, I have a piece of Poetry to read to you.'
(THE HOUSE AT POOH CORNER, pages 161–62)

Excitement, *Refer:* **Braces,** *especially* **Really** *blue ones.*

Exercises, Stoutness, *Refer:* **Stoutness Exercises.**

Expedition, *noun:* A long line of those who are not necessarily sure they should be in it, but nonetheless have to join it in order to discover whether it leads to anywhere they want to go.

'We are all going on an Expedition,' said Christopher Robin, as he got up and brushed himself. 'Thank you, Pooh . . . .

We're going to discover the North Pole.'

'Oh!' said Pooh again. 'What *is* the North Pole?' he asked.

'It's just a thing you discover,' said Christopher Robin carelessly, not being quite sure himself.

'Oh! I see,' said Pooh. 'Are bears any good at discovering it?'

'Of course they are. And Rabbit and Kanga and all of you. It's an Expedition. That's what an Expedition means. A long line of everybody.'

(WINNIE-THE-POOH, pages 101–02)

See also: **Adventure;** *and* **Confused Noise.**

Explore, *Refer:* **What-Shall-I-Do-About-You-Know-What.**

Expo, *mumble-noun:* An **Expedition*,** but one you can't pronounce properly (and don't want to go on).

'What I say,' said Eeyore, 'is that it's unsettling. I didn't want to come on this Expo – what Pooh said. I only came to oblige. But here I am.'

(WINNIE-THE-POOH, page 104)

See Also: **Confused Noise;** *and* **Expotition.**

Expotition, *noun*: Alternative pronunciation of **Expedition***, but more accurately refers to a long line of people in a boat, usually on voyages of discovery in which, it is hoped by all concerned, nothing Fierce is discovered. Term rarely used.

The first person [Pooh] met was Rabbit . . . .
'We're all going on an Expotition with Christopher Robin!'
'What is it when we're on it?'
'A sort of boat, I think,' said Pooh.
'Oh! that sort.'

(WINNIE-THE-POOH, pages 102–03)

'Oh! Piglet,' said Pooh excitedly, 'we're going on an Expotition, all of us, with things to eat. To discover something.'

'To discover what?' said Piglet anxiously.

(**WINNIE-THE-POOH, page 103**)

See Also: **Accident; Boat;** *and* **Expo.**

Extract of Malt, *Refer:* Medicine.

Favourite Size, *Refer:* **Size, favourite.**

Fierce Animal, *phrasal noun:* Any animal who displays a certain lack of Friendliness, and, sometimes, outright Rudeness, to the well-being of your person. Avoid these animals.

Fiercer Animal, *phrasal noun:* **Fierce Animal*** (only Fiercer). *Example:* **Jagular**.

Fiercer Animal, Deprived of Its Young, *phrasal noun:* Any animal who intentionally or otherwise worries, frightens, or intimidates Very Small Animals, especially Childless Very Small Animals, for no other reason than that Fiercer Animals are Bad Tempered at the best of times and become Really Bad Tempered when their Young disappear, hide, or are lost.

'There's just one thing,' said Piglet, fidgeting a bit. 'I was talking to Christopher Robin, and he said that a Kanga was Generally Regarded as One of the Fiercer Animals. I am not frightened of Fierce Animals in the ordinary way, but it is well known that, if One of the Fiercer Animals is Deprived of Its Young, it becomes as fierce as Two of the Fiercer Animals . . . .'

'Piglet,' said Rabbit, taking out a pencil, and licking the end of it, 'you haven't any pluck.'

'It is hard to be brave,' said Piglet, sniffing slightly, 'when you're only a Very Small Animal.'
(**WINNIE-THE-POOH, pages 84–85**)

See Also: **Affectionate Disposition; Aha!; Good-Bye-And-Thank-You-For-A-Nice-Time;** *and* **Lost.**

Fierce with Pigs, *Refer:* **Fond of Pigs.**

Flashed Past, *Refer:* **No Exchange of Thought.**

Floating Bear, The, *nautical noun:* Pooh's biggest jar, without honey inside, of course, and his unstablest boat. Also known as the **Accident*,** depending on whether it or Pooh is underneath.

He said to himself:

'If a bottle can float, then a jar can float, and if a jar floats, I can sit on the top of it, if it's a very big jar.'

So he took his biggest jar, and corked it up. 'All boats have to have a name,' he said, 'so I shall call mine *The Floating Bear*.' And with these words he dropped his boat into the water and jumped in after it.

For a little while Pooh and *The Floating Bear* were uncertain as to which of them was meant to be on the top.

(WINNIE-THE-POOH, pages 123–24)

See Also: **Umbrella.**

Fluff, *noun:* What Bears think with – well, sort of think with – when a little bit hasn't slipped into their ears or something. That is, what Bears use instead of **Brain***.

Pooh shook his head.

'I don't know,' he said. 'It just didn't. What are we talking about?'

'Pooh,' said Piglet reproachfully, 'haven't you been listening to what Rabbit was saying?'

'I listened, but I had a small piece of fluff in my ear. Could you say it again, please, Rabbit?'

(THE HOUSE AT POOH CORNER, page 108)

'Owl,' said Rabbit shortly, 'you and I have brains. The others have fluff. If there is any thinking to be done in the Forest – and when I say thinking I mean *thinking* – you and I must do it.'

'Yes,' said Owl. 'I was.'

(THE HOUSE AT POOH CORNER, page 76)

Fly, *verb*: To do what Owl does, because he has the **Necessary Dorsal Muscles*,** which is to move through the air using wings rather than having to walk like other animals (Owl can walk, but he can fly much better), and, in fact, flying is what Owl does best (besides being able to talk using **Long Words*** and Very Long Sentences). Except, Pooh has been known to fly using **Balloons*,** which makes you wonder what Owl goes on about.

The next moment the day became very bothering indeed, because Pooh was so busy not looking where he was going that he stepped on a piece of the Forest which had been left out by mistake; and he only just had time to think to himself: 'I'm flying. What Owl does. I wonder how you stop –' when he stopped.

Bump!

(THE HOUSE AT POOH CORNER, page 38)

'Could you fly up to the letter-box with Piglet on your back?' he asked . . . .

Owl explained about the Necessary Dorsal Muscles.

(THE HOUSE AT POOH CORNER, page 137)

. . . . In jumped Piglet into Kanga's pocket . . . .

'Well, we must be getting home,' said Kanga. 'Good-bye, Pooh.' And in three large jumps she was gone.

Pooh looked after her as she went.

'I wish I could jump like that,' he thought. 'Some can and some can't. That's how it is.'

But there were moments when Piglet wished that Kanga couldn't. Often when he had had a long walk home through the Forest, he had wished that he were a bird; but now he thought jerkily to himself at the bottom of Kanga's pocket,

'If this is flying I shall never really take to it.'

And as he went up in the air, he said, '*Ooooooo!*' and as he came down he said, '*Ow!*' And he was saying,' '*Ooooooo-ow, Ooooooo-ow, Ooooooo-ow*' all the way to Kanga's house.

(WINNIE-THE-POOH, page 92)

Refer: **Jumping.**

Fond of Pigs, *phrasal adjective:* Not the same as Friendly to Pigs, but definitely the opposite of Fierce with Pigs. *Fond of* Pigs means not only that you like to *be with* Pigs, but also that you like to *eat* Pigs. The usage is similar to the expression found in 'Piglet is fond of haycorns.' However, while Piglet may feel only warmth toward haycorns, *they* might not be too thrilled about it.

By and by Piglet woke up. As soon as he woke he said to himself, 'Oh!' Then he said bravely, 'Yes,' and then, still more bravely, 'Quite so.' But he didn't feel very brave, for the word which was really jiggeting about in his brain was 'Heffalumps.'

What was a Heffalump like?

Was it Fierce?

Did it come when you whistled? And *how* did it come?

Was it Fond of Pigs at all?

If it was Fond of Pigs, did it make any difference *what sort of Pig?* . . . .

[Piglet] didn't know the answers to any of these questions.

(WINNIE-THE-POOH, page 60)

See Also: **Little Something (to Revive Oneself)**

Food, *noun:* Things You Eat. (All animals must decide what sort of Things to Eat and especially in what Quantity, and giving consideration to their individual Shape and Appetite.)

Foolish, *Refer:* **Foolish And Uncomfortable;** *and* **No Brain.**

Foolish and Deluded, *Refer:* **No Brain.**

Foolish and Uncomfortable, *phrasal adjective:* **1** what an animal feels when it wants to run away (without knowing the why of it). **2** what all Sailors feel on a bad day in the middle of a storm in the middle of the sea when they realize they still don't know why they bothered to run away to *this*.

> Then Piglet saw what a Foolish Piglet he had been, and he was so ashamed of himself that he ran straight off home and went to bed with a headache.
>
> **(WINNIE-THE-POOH, page 64)**

> Piglet looked up, and looked away again. And he felt so Foolish and Uncomfortable that he had almost decided to run away to Sea and be a Sailor.
>
> **(THE HOUSE AT POOH CORNER, page 50)**

F. O. P., *abbreviation:* **Friend of Piglet*.**
Refer: **Winnie-The-Pooh, Honorific Titles Thereof.**

Friday, *noun:* The name for that day, past or future, in which something occurs that is of significance to whatever is happening today.

Once upon a time, a very long time ago now, about last Friday, Winnie-the-Pooh lived in a forest all by himself.

(**WINNIE-THE-POOH, page 2**)

Piglet scratched his ear in a nice sort of way, and said that he had nothing to do until Friday, and would be delighted to come.

(**WINNIE-THE-POOH, page 33**)

Friendly Day, *phrasal noun:* One of those days in which you relax and enjoy the **Company*** of Friends (who, by definition, therefore, are rather Fond of Eating).

'Let's go and see *everybody,*' said Pooh. 'Because when you've been walking in the wind for miles, and you suddenly go into somebody's house, and he says, "Hallo, Pooh, you're just in time for a little smackerel of something," and you are, then it's what I call a Friendly Day.'
(THE HOUSE AT POOH CORNER, page 126)

Refer: **Food.**

Friend of Piglet, *Refer:* **Winnie-The-Pooh, Honorific Titles Thereof.**

Friends-and-Relations, *phrasal noun:* **1** all those to whom Rabbit owes some responsibility because, well, someone has to be Responsible, and it may as well be Rabbit. **2** hence, friends-and-relations are all those folk to whom you are responsible because, well, why not you (after all, most friends and most relations are far too busy).

'What I came to say was: Have you seen Small about?'
'I don't think so,' said Pooh. And then, after

thinking a little more, he said: 'Who is Small?'

'One of my friends-and-relations,' said Rabbit carelessly.

This didn't help Pooh much, because Rabbit had so many friends-and-relations, and of such different sorts and sizes, that he didn't know whether he ought to be looking for Small at the top of an oak-tree or in the petal of a buttercup.

'I haven't seen anybody today,' said Pooh, 'not so as to say "Hello, Small!" to. Did you want him for anything?'

'I *don't* want him,' said Rabbit. 'But it is always useful to know where a friend-and-relation *is,* whether you want him or whether you don't.'

(THE HOUSE AT POOH CORNER, page 36)

See Also: **Captainish.**

Funny Feeling, *phrasal noun:* That feeling that tells you that it is time to head for the **Food***** cupboard (either yours or somebody else's).

It was a warm day, and he had a long way to go. He hadn't gone more than half-way when a sort of funny feeling began to creep over him.

It began at the tip of his nose and trickled all through him and out at the soles of his feet. It was just as if somebody inside him were saying, 'Now then, Pooh, time for a little something.'

(**WINNIE-THE-POOH**, pages 71–72)

See Also: **Eleven O'clockish;** *and* **Home.**

Gg

Games, *Refer:* **Poohsticks.**

Generally Regarded, *phrasal adverb:* Meaning that everybody who knows about it agrees about it.

Giving In, *phrasal verb:* To show a lack of **Pluck*,** which isn't necessarily a bad thing if you are a Very Small Animal.

'We'll go out, Piglet, and sing my song to Eeyore.'

'Which song, Pooh?' . . . .

The wind had dropped, and the snow, tired of rushing round in circles trying to catch itself up, now fluttered gently down until it found a place on which to rest, and sometimes the place was Pooh's nose and sometimes it wasn't, and in a little while Piglet was wearing a white muffler round his neck and feeling more snowy behind the ears than he had ever felt before.

'Pooh,' he said at last, and a little timidly, because he didn't want Pooh to think he was Giving In, 'I was just wondering. How would it be if we went home now and *practised* your song and then sang it to Eeyore tomorrow – or – or the next day, when we happen to see him?'
(THE HOUSE AT POOH CORNER, pages 3–4)

See Also: **Blinch.**

Gloomy, *Refer:* **Very Sad Condition.**

Gloomy Place, *geographical highlight:* Where Eeyore lives, because that's the sort of donkey he is.

> By this time they were getting near Eeyore's Gloomy Place, which was where he lived.
> **(The House At Pooh Corner, page 7)**

See Also: **Very Sad Condition.**

Goloptious, *adjective (from the noun* **golop***):* Describes how a pot, jar, or any container of food is just right for you to push your tongue out and (fondly) curl it around the bottom (of the pot, jar, or container) to get the very last and very best morsel.

> *It's very, very funny,*
> *'Cos I know I had some honey;*
> *'Cos it had a label on,*
> *Saying* HUNNY.
>
> *A goloptious full-up pot too,*
> *And I don't know where it's got to.*
> **(WINNIE-THE-POOH, page 57)**

See Also: **Bear, Eating Habits Thereof.**

Gon Out, *phrasal verb* (perfect tense): From of *gone out* used and understood by **Backsons***.

> GON OUT
>
> BACKSON
>
> BISY
>
> BACKSON.
>
> C. R.

(THE HOUSE AT POOH CORNER, page 75)

See Also: **Spelling.**

Good-bye-and-Thank-You-for-a-Nice-Time, *correctly polite final words*: The very least comment any polite guest should make on departing (whether the visit was enjoyable or not).

> [Small] had been staying with Christopher Robin for a few seconds, and he started round a gorse-bush for exercise, but instead of coming back the other way, as expected, he hadn't, so nobody knew where he was.
>
> 'I expect he's just gone home,' said Christopher Robin to Rabbit.
>
> 'Did he say Good-bye-and-thank-you-for-a-nice-time?' said Rabbit.
>
> 'He's only just said how-do-you-do,' said Christopher Robin.

(THE HOUSE AT POOH CORNER, pages 45–46)

Good Hum, *Refer:* **Hum.**

Good Thing, *noun:* Whatever happens to you that is pleasing and satisfying without involving **Food*** (in which case it would be the **Best Thing***). A Good Thing happens when you weren't expecting it but are jolly happy it does. One can do a Good Thing, but not with any forethought. In fact, having **Brain*** can interfere with enjoying life's little good things.

> 'Well,' said Pooh, 'we keep looking for Home and not finding it, so I thought that if we looked for this Pit, we'd be sure not to find it, which would be a Good Thing, because then we might find something that we *weren't* looking for, which might just be what we *were* looking for, really.'
>
> **(THE HOUSE AT POOH CORNER, page 121)**

> [Piglet] thought to himself . . . . 'There's Kanga. She isn't Clever, Kanga isn't, but she would be so anxious about Roo that she would do a Good Thing to Do without thinking about it.'
>
> **(WINNIE-THE-POOH, pages 118–119)**

See Also: **Home.**

Gorse-Bush, *Refer:* **Ambush.**

Grandfathers, *venerable beings:* Relatives about whom one may feel affectionate even though they have a funny name or two. *Refer:* **Trespassers Will.**

Grandfather T.W., *Refer:* **Trespassers William.**

Grand Idea, *phrasal noun:* **1** quite specifically, this was the notion of building Eeyore a house without asking him, which led to an **Awful Mistake*.** **2** generally, while the idea that every animal requires a house can be said to be a Good Idea, a Grand Idea is one in which you decide to build a house for another animal because you consider his present living circumstances inadequate. This can lead to Awful Mistakes, although there is a strong chance you will probably win a great many architectural awards.

'*You* have a house, Piglet, and I have a house, and they are very good houses. And Christopher Robin has a house, and Owl and Kanga and Rabbit have houses, and even Rabbit's friends and relations have houses or somethings, but poor Eeyore has nothing. So what I've been thinking is: Let's build him a house.'

'That,' said Piglet, 'is a Grand Idea. Where shall we build it?'

'We will build it here,' said Pooh.
(THE HOUSE AT POOH CORNER, page 7)

Great Help, *noun:* How to describe someone who is very **Useful***.

Grrrr-oppp-ptschschschz, *exclamation* and *unrequited sigh:* A phrase that captures all the heartache and pain that a simple expression of endearment can bring when it is misunderstood.

> Rabbit became very important suddenly.
>
> 'Tigger,' he said solemnly, 'what happened just now?'
>
> 'Just when?' said Tigger a little uncomfortably.
>
> 'When you bounced Eeyore into the river.'
>
> 'I didn't bounce him.'
>
> 'You bounced me,' said Eeyore gruffly.
>
> 'I didn't really. I had a cough, and I happened to be behind Eeyore, and I said *"Grrrr-oppp-ptschschschz."*'

(THE HOUSE AT POOH CORNER, page 101)

See Also: **Boff;** *and* **Coffy.**

Hh

HB, *Refer:* **B.**

Head Above Water, *Refer:* **Sudden and Temporary Immersion (the Important Thing to Do).**

Headache, *noun:* You say you have this when either (1) you wish to avoid the possibility of a larger animal interfering with your person; or (2) you wish to avoid the embarrassment of another animal seeing your person (no matter how much a **Good Thing*** it might be if it did).

> [Piglet was thinking] . . . . he was going to see his first Heffalump in about an hour from now! . . . . Suppose Heffalumps were Very Fierce with Pigs *and* Bears? Wouldn't it be better to

pretend that he had a headache, and couldn't go up to the Six Pine Trees this morning?
(WINNIE-THE-POOH, pages 61–62)

See Also: **Foolish** *and* **Uncomfortable**.

Hearing, Method Advanced by Eeyore, *useful tip:* A simple but effective means of hearing better by pushing your ear forward with your foot. While this method (advanced by Eeyore) may *appear* rather physically exacting, no animal should be hesitant to go to great lengths to hear what another is saying. After all, it might have to do with something important (like 'Hallo! Did you know your tail is missing?').

'Just say that again,' [Eeyore said to Piglet].
'Many hap –'
'Wait a moment.'
Balancing on three legs, he began to bring his fourth leg very cautiously up to his ear. 'I did this yesterday,' he explained, as he fell down for the third time. 'It's quite easy. It's so as I can hear better . . . There, that's done it! Now then, what were you saying?' He pushed his ear forward with his hoof.
(WINNIE-THE-POOH, page 76)

See Also: **Little Bit Extra.**

Hearty Joke, *phrasal noun:* When someone (or a collection of someones) is (*are,* if there are someones) out to make a fool of you, or at least have a good guffaw at your misfortune.

And out floated Eeyore.

'Eeyore!' cried everybody.

Looking very calm, very dignified, with his legs in the air, came Eeyore from beneath the bridge . . . .

With a shout they rushed off the bridge, and pushed and pulled at him; and soon he was standing among them again on dry land.

'Oh, Eeyore, you *are* wet!' said Piglet, feeling him.

Eeyore shook himself, and asked somebody to explain to Piglet what happened when you had been inside a river for quite a long time . . . .

'How did you fall in, Eeyore?' asked Rabbit, as he dried him with Piglet's handkerchief.

'I didn't,' said Eeyore . . . .

'But, Eeyore,' said Pooh, 'was it a Joke, or an Accident? I mean –'

'I didn't stop to ask, Pooh. Even at the very

bottom of the river I didn't stop to say to myself, "Is this a Hearty Joke, or is it the Merest Accident?" I just floated to the surface, and said to myself, "It's wet." If you know what I mean.'

(THE HOUSE AT POOH CORNER, pages 94, 98–100)
NOTE: If Hearty Jokes persist, make friends with a **Fierce Animal*** or, in extreme cases, two **Fiercer Animals***.

Heff, *Refer:* **Heffalump, Alternative Nomenclature.**

Heffalump, *noun:* **1** a Very Large Animal whose Presence is felt in the Forest, but whose Actual Presence is Rarely Enjoyed. **2** any Very Large Animal whom you know to be lurking somewhere (and you are a little Cautious of meeting it, but at the same time you would so much like just to have a *safe* glimpse of it).

One day, when Christopher Robin and Winnie-the-Pooh and Piglet were all talking together, Christopher Robin finished the mouthful he was eating and said carelessly: 'I saw a Heffalump to-day, Piglet.'

'What was it doing?' asked Piglet.

'Just lumping along,' said Christopher Robin. 'I don't think it saw *me*.'

'I saw one once,' said Piglet. 'At least, I think I did,' he said. 'Only perhaps it wasn't.'

'So did I,' said Pooh, wondering what a Heffalump was like.

'You don't often see them,' said Christopher Robin carelessly.

'Not now,' said Piglet.

'Not at this time of year,' said Pooh.

(WINNIE-THE-POOH, pages 51–52)

Heffalump, Alternative Nomenclature:
Hoffalump (Herrible), Horralump (Hellible), and, Hellerump (Hoffable) are terms used by Smaller Animals when the experience of meeting a Heffalump is all a bit too much. The correct way to *address* a Heffalump is 'Sir' or 'Ma'am.'

'Help, help!' cried Piglet, 'a Heffalump, a Horrible Heffalump!' and he scampered off as hard as he could, still crying out, 'Help, help, a Herrible Hoffalump! Hoff, Hoff, a Hellible Horralump! Holl, Holl, a Hoffable Hellerump!' And he didn't stop crying and scampering until he got to Christopher Robin's house . . . .

'Heff,' said Piglet, breathing so hard that he could hardly speak, 'a Hell – a Heff – a Heffalump.'

(**WINNIE-THE-POOH, page 63**)

Heffalump: How to Upset, *Refer:* **Ho-*ho***!

Heffalump Trap (for Poohs), *phrasal noun:* A trap set by a Heffalump for the purpose of capturing Poohs and Piglets.

'What's happened?' said Pooh. 'Where are we?'

'I think we're in a sort of Pit. I was walking along, looking for somebody, and then suddenly I wasn't any more, and just when I got up to see where I was, something fell on me. And it was you.'

'So it was,' said Pooh.

'Yes,' said Piglet. 'Pooh,' he went on nervously, and came a little closer, 'do you think we're in a trap?'

Pooh hadn't thought about it at all, but now he nodded. For suddenly he remembered how he and Piglet had once made a Pooh Trap for Heffalumps, and he guessed what had happened. He and Piglet had fallen into a Heffalump Trap for Poohs! That was what it was.

(**THE HOUSE AT POOH CORNER, page 41**)

See Also: **Cunning Trap; Underneath;** *and* **Very Deep Pit.**

Heffalumping, *verb:* **1** specifically, what Piglet believes a Heffalump does when hunting piglets; *noun:* **2** however, the term can be used to refer to whatever you believe proves your belief that something really is as you believe it. The illogic goes something like this:

(1) I expect a Heffalump (or whatever).

(2) I hear a noise that possibly could be made by a Heffalump (or whatever).

(3) Therefore ipso facto there is a Heffalump (or whatever).

> At first [Piglet thought] that there wouldn't be a Heffalump in the Trap, and then he thought that there would, and as he got nearer he was *sure* that there would, because he could hear it heffalumping about it like anything.
>
> **(WINNIE-THE-POOH, page 61)**

Hellerump, *Refer:* **Heffalump, Alternative Nomenclature.**

Hellible, *adjective:* Descriptive word for a Heffalump. *Refer:* **Heffalump, Alternative Nomenclature.**

Henry Pootel, *abbreviation:* Shortened form of the name **Pootel*.**

Herbaceous Backson, *noun:* One of two types of **Backson***, noted for their inability to spell properly.

See Also: **Gon Out.**

Herrible, *adjective:* Descriptive term for a Heffalump. *Refer:* **Heffalump, Alternative Nomenclature.**

Hipy Papy Bthuthdth Thuthda Bthuthdy, *incorrectly spelt phrasal noun:* Literally, what Owl believes is the spelling of 'Happy Birthday' (which just goes to show that **Spelling*** isn't everything).

> So Owl wrote ... and this is what he wrote:
> HIPY PAPY BTHUTHDTH THUTHDA
> BTHUTHDY.
> Pooh looked on admiringly.
> 'I'm just saying "A Happy Birthday,"' said Owl carelessly.
> 'It's a nice long one,' said Pooh, very much impressed by it.
> 'Well, *actually,* of course, I'm saying "A Very Happy Birthday with love from Pooh." Naturally it takes a

good deal of pencil to say a long thing like that.'
'Oh, I see,' said Pooh.
(**WINNIE-THE-POOH, pages 74–75**)

See Also: **Brain;** *and* **Respect.**

Hoff, Hoff, *meaningless terror-induced exclamation:* What you might say when being chased by a **Hellible* Horralump***.

Hoffable, *adjective:* Descriptive term for a Heffalump. *Refer:* **Heffalump, Alternative Nomenclature.**

Hoffalump, *Refer:* **Heffalump, Alternative Nomenclature.**

Ho-*ho*!, *exclamation:* **1** specifically, what a Heffalump says when it comes across you unexpectedly. **2** generally, can refer to that moment you come across something or someone unexpectedly and you are completely at a loss as to what to say but you know you should say something. Typically, 'Ho-ho!' ends all possible future conversation.

'What happens when the Heffalump comes?' asked Piglet trembling . . . .
'He'll notice *me,* and I shall notice *him,*' said Pooh, thinking it out. 'We'll

notice each other for a long time, and then he'll say: "Ho-*ho*!"'

Piglet shivered a little at the thought of that 'Ho-*ho*!' and his ears began to twitch.

'W-what will *you* say?' he asked.

Pooh tried to think of something he would say, but the more he thought, the more he felt that there *is* no real answer to 'Ho-*ho*!' said by a Heffalump in that sort of voice this Heffalump was going to say it in.

(The House At Pooh Corner, pages 41–42)

Compare: **Aha!; Bother!;** *and* **Hush!**

Holl, Holl, *meaningless terror-induced exclamation*: What you might say, when not saying **Hoff, Hoff*,** as a **Hoffable* Hellerump*** is chasing you.

See Also: **Heffalump, Alternative Nomenclature.**

Home, *noun*: Where your **Food*** lives (so you live there too).

'I just thought,' said Pooh. 'Now then, Piglet, let's go home.'

'But, Pooh,' cried Piglet, all excited, 'do you know the way?'

'No,' said Pooh. 'But there are twelve pots

of honey in my cupboard, and they've been calling to me for hours. I couldn't hear them properly before, because Rabbit *would* talk, but if nobody says anything except those twelve pots, I *think,* Piglet, I shall know where they're calling from. Come on.'

They walked off together; and for a long time, Piglet said nothing, so as not to interrupt the pots; and then suddenly he made a squeaky noise . . . and an oo-noise . . . because now he began to know where he was.

(**THE HOUSE AT POOH CORNER, pages 121–22**)

See Also: **Funny Feeling.**

Honey, *noun:* Alternative spelling of **Hunny*.**

Hoosh, *verb:* **1** to help someone out of a difficult situation by overenthusiastic use of force. **2** more precisely, to come to the *vigorous* aid of someone without his knowing consent.

'Well done, Pooh,' said Rabbit kindly. 'That was a good idea of ours.'

'What was?' asked Eeyore.

'Hooshing you to the bank like that.'

'*Hooshing* me?' said Eeyore in surprise.

'Hooshing *me*? You didn't think I was *hooshed,* did you? I dived. Pooh dropped a large stone on me, and so as not to be struck heavily on the chest, I dived and swam to the bank.'

'You didn't really,' whispered Piglet to Pooh, so as to comfort him.

'I didn't *think* I did,' said Pooh anxiously.

(THE HOUSE AT POOH CORNER, page 99)

See Also: **Awful Mistake; Grand Idea;** *and* **Hearty Joke.**

Horralump, *Refer:* **Heffalump, Alternative Nomenclature.**

Hostile Intent, *phrasal noun*: Said of animals who are Purposely Unfriendly to Others (but not to one another, as they always seem to go round in small groups).

So they went on, feeling just a little anxious now, in case the three animals in front of them were of Hostile Intent.

(WINNIE-THE-POOH, page 35)

See Also: **Wizzle;** *and* **Woozle.**

House, *Refer:* **Awful Mistake; Grand Idea; Home;** *and* **Noble Thing.**

How, *noun:* A philosophical term (developed by Eeyore) that encapsulates the existential reality confronting those animals who have pondered the mystery of Life and have accepted the notion that Existence Is, but find problematic the question 'How should I truly exist?' Or something like it.

So when Winnie-the-Pooh came stumping along, Eeyore was very glad to be able to stop thinking for a little, in order to say 'How do you do?' in a gloomy manner to him.

'And how are you?' said Winnie-the-Pooh.

Eeyore shook his head from side to side.

'Not very how,' he said. 'I don't seem to have felt at all how for a long time.'

(Winnie-the-Pooh, page 40)

See Also: **Inasmuch As Which;** *and* **Mean Anything.**

How Like Them, *phrasal noun* and *interjection:* Refers to the situation in which you find that your lowly expectations of others are totally justified.

> So Eeyore stood there, gazing sadly at the ground, and Winnie-the-Pooh walked all round him once.
>
> 'Why, what's happened to your tail?' he said in surprise.
>
> 'What *has* happened to it?' said Eeyore.
>
> 'It isn't there!'
>
> 'Are you sure?' . . . .
>
> 'Of course I'm right,' said Pooh . . . .
>
> 'You must have left it somewhere,' said Winnie-the-Pooh.
>
> 'Somebody must have taken it,' said Eeyore. 'How Like Them,' he added, after a long silence.

(WINNIE-THE-POOH, pages 40–42)

See Also: **No Wonder.**

Hum, *noun:* **1** a verse or two that expresses, with feeling or imagination, just how good life is when you have a **Positively Startling Lack of Brain***. Winnie-the-Pooh does very good hums (usually short); *verb:* **2** to *allow* verses or hums to come out from wherever it is they come from.

'But it isn't Easy,' said Pooh to himself, as he looked at what had once been Owl's House.

'Because Poetry and Hums aren't things which you get, they're things which get *you*. And all you can do is to go where they can find you.'

He waited hopefully . . . .

(THE HOUSE AT POOH CORNER, pages 144–45)

First [Pooh] thought that he would knock very loudly just to make *quite* sure . . . and while he waited for Piglet not to answer, he jumped up and down to keep warm, and a hum came suddenly into his head.

(THE HOUSE AT POOH CORNER, pages 1–2)

'There are seven verses in it.'

'Seven?' said Piglet as carelessly as he

could. 'You don't often get *seven* verses in a Hum, do you, Pooh?'

'Never,' said Pooh. 'I don't suppose it's *ever* been heard of before.'

(THE HOUSE AT POOH CORNER, page 149)

Compare: **Loud Sounds.**
See Also: **Poem.**

Hunger, *Refer:* **Funny Feeling.**

Hunny, *noun:* **1** alternative spelling of *honey,* and derived from the verb *to hunny; verb:* **2** to be in the process of making honey, which is done by **Bees*** (genus *Apis*), which gather nectar from flowers, digest it, and regurgitate it into honeycombs, so that bears can then eat it at their leisure (in fact, bears will eat *at* anything, especially other people's tables).

As soon as [Pooh] got home, he went to the larder; and he stood on a chair, and took down a very large jar of honey from the top shelf. It had HUNNY written on it.

(WINNIE-THE-POOH, page 55)

First of all [Pooh] said to himself: 'That buzzing-noise means something. You don't get a buzzing-noise like that, just buzzing and buzzing, without its meaning something. If there's a buzzing-noise, somebody's making a buzzing-noise, and the only reason for making a buzzing-noise that *I* know of is because you're a bee.'

Then he thought another long time, and said: 'And the only reason for being a bee that I know of is making honey.'

And then he got up, and said: 'And the only reason for making honey is so as *I* can eat it.'

(**WINNIE-THE-POOH, pages 3–4**)

'Well,' said Pooh, 'if I plant a honeycomb outside my house, then it will grow up into a beehive.'

Piglet wasn't quite sure about this.

'Or a *piece* of a honeycomb,' said Pooh, 'so as not to waste too much. Only then I might only get a piece of a beehive, and it might be the wrong piece, where the bees were buzzing and not hunnying. Bother.'

(**THE HOUSE AT POOH CORNER, pages 56– 57**)

See Also: **Bear, Eating Habits Thereof.**

Hunt, *verb*: To look for whatever it is you are supposed to find, without being told what it is yet.

[Pooh] thought he would begin the Hunt by looking for Piglet, and asking him what they were looking for before he looked for it.

(The House At Pooh Corner, page 37)

Pooh was walking round and round in a circle, thinking of something else, and when Piglet called to him, he just went on walking.

'Hallo!' said Piglet, 'what are *you* doing?'

'Hunting,' said Pooh.

'Hunting what?'

'Tracking something,' said Winnie-the-Pooh very mysteriously.

'Tracking what?' said Piglet, coming closer.

'That's just what I ask myself. I ask myself, What?'

'What do you think you'll answer?'

'I shall have to wait until I catch up with it,' said Winnie-the-Pooh.

(WINNIE-THE-POOH, pages 31–32)

See Also: **Scerching;** *and* **Tracking Something.**

Hush!, *imperative verb:* Exactly equivalent in meaning and content to: 'Be quiet! I'm very nervous and I can't think if you all chatter on so happily.' However, if everyone is saying 'Hush! Hush!' to nobody in particular and only because suddenly everyone is getting a little nervous, it can be an unpleasant choice of word to throw at Very Sensitive Types. It is strongly recommended that Small Animals avoid strong language and say no more (and we mean *no more*) than **'Bother!*'** at *any* time.

'Hush!' said Christopher Robin turning round to Pooh, 'we're just coming to a Dangerous Place.'

'Hush!' said Pooh turning round quickly to Piglet.

'Hush! said Kanga to Owl, while Roo said 'Hush!' several times to himself very quietly.

'Hush!' said Owl to Eeyore.

'*Hush!*' said Eeyore in a terrible voice to all Rabbit's friends-and-relations, and 'Hush!' they said hastily to each other all down the line, until it got to the last one of all. And the last and smallest friend-and-relation was so upset to find that the whole Expotition was saying 'Hush!' to *him,* that he buried himself head downwards in a crack in the ground, and stayed there for two days until the danger was over, and then went home in a great hurry, and lived quietly with his Aunt ever-afterwards. His name was Alexander Beetle.

(**WINNIE-THE-POOH, page 107**)

See Also: **Aha!;** *and* **Ho-ho!**

Idea, *Refer:* **Thingish;** *and* **Very Good Idea.**

Immersion, *Refer:* **Sudden** *and* **Temporary Immersion (the Important Thing to Do).**

See Also: **Bath;** *and* **Washing Nonsense (Behind the Ears).**

Important Feeling, *Refer:* **Captainish;** *and* **Funny Feeling.**

Important Thing, *noun:* Opposite to **Best Thing*** and **Good Thing*,** and is *anything* you expect, assume, understand, or consider very necessary. In fact, it is so necessary that nothing else should be done or considered. Smaller Animals who are curious as to what constitutes an Important Thing can be guided by how **Serious*** it is. Important Things are always serious.

'We've come to wish you a Very Happy Thursday,' said Pooh, when he had gone in and out once or twice just to make sure he *could* get out again.

'Why, what's going to happen on Thursday?' asked Rabbit, and when Pooh had explained, and Rabbit, whose life was made up of Important Things, said, 'Oh, I thought you'd really come about something,' they sat down for a little . . . and by-and-by Pooh and Piglet went on again. The wind was behind them now, so they didn't have to shout.

'Rabbit's clever,' said Pooh thoughtfully.

(THE HOUSE AT POOH CORNER, page 127)

Refer: **Sudden and Temporary Immersion (the Important Thing to Do).**

Inasmuch As Which, *complicated adverb used as noun:* A philosophical term similar in usage to **How*** but more pronounced. When an animal might ask *how* one ought to live one's life, *inasmuch as which* refers to the specificity of the *how*. In other words, should one live for thistles (that is, is the pursuit of thistles the appropriate raison d'être of life), and if so, *inasmuch as which,* what type of thistles?

The Old Grey Donkey, Eeyore, stood by himself in a thistly corner of the forest, his front feet well apart, his head on one side, and thought about things. Sometimes he thought sadly to himself, 'Why?' and sometimes he thought, 'Wherefore?' and sometimes he thought, 'Inasmuch as which?' – and sometimes he didn't quite know what he was thinking about.

(**WINNIE-THE-POOH, pages 39-40**)

See Also: **Mean Anything.**

Instigorate, *verb:* To become **Educated***, which is whatever you do with **Knowledge*** once you get it.

'What does Christopher Robin do in the mornings?' said Eeyore. 'He learns. He becomes Educated. He instigorates – I *think* that is the word he mentioned, but I may be referring to something else – he instigorates Knowledge. In my small way I also, if I have the word right, am – am doing what he does.'

(**THE HOUSE AT POOH CORNER**, page 87)

See Also: **A;** *and* **Learn in Books.**

Interesting Anecdote, *phrasal noun:* Something that Owl tells which is of particular interest to himself, but whether it is mildly exciting to anyone else is difficult to say (without really offending Owl).

Owl was telling Kanga an Interesting Anecdote full of long words like Encyclopaedia and Rhododendron to which Kanga wasn't listening.

(**WINNIE-THE-POOH**, page 110)

Issue, *verb:* **1** to give out or provide; **2** (to Bears like Pooh) to sneeze; *noun:* **3** (to Bears like Pooh) a sneeze.

'The thing to do is as follows. First, Issue a Reward. Then –'

'Just a moment,' said Pooh, holding up his paw. '*What* do we do to this — what you were saying? You sneezed just as you were going to tell me.'

'I *didn't* sneeze.'

'Yes, you did, Owl.'

'Excuse me, Pooh, I didn't. You can't sneeze without knowing it.'

'Well, you can't know it without something having been sneezed.'

'What I *said* was, "First *Issue* a Reward."'

'You are doing it again,' said Pooh sadly.

(WINNIE-THE-POOH, pages 45–46)

See Also: **Sqoze.**

It Explains Everything, *exclamation of despair:* What once before was unexplainably depressing and is now totally depressing.

'That Accounts for a Good Deal,' said Eeyore gloomily. 'It Explains Everything. No Wonder.'

(WINNIE-THE-POOH, page 42)

Jagular, *noun:* A Dropping Animal. *Refer:* **Very Good Dropper.**

Joke, *Refer:* **Hearty Joke** (as opposed to MEREST ACCIDENT).

Jostle, *noun:* A walk that is neither a **Short Walk*** nor a **Thinking Walk*,** but more a confused and crowded walk.

> Christopher Robin jumped up.
> 'Come on, Pooh,' he said.
> 'Come on, Tigger!' cried Roo.
> 'Shall we go, Owl?' said Rabbit . . . .
> Eeyore waved them back.
> 'Christopher Robin and I are going for a Short Walk,' he said, 'not a Jostle. If he likes to

bring Pooh and Piglet with him, I shall be glad of their company, but one must be able to Breathe.'

(**THE HOUSE AT POOH CORNER, pages 155–56**)

See Also: **Company; Shortness of Breath;** *and* **Spreading.**

Jump, *verb:* **1** to project oneself upward and onward, whether for the purpose of moving along (instead of walking), fun, or to avoid danger quickly; *adjective* (JUMPING): **2** having the ability to project oneself upward and onward; *variant adjective* (JUMPY): **3** indecisive and nervous (about projecting oneself upward and onward for fun or to avoid danger quickly).

Pooh, who had decided to be a Kanga, was still at the sandy place on the top of the Forest, practising jumps.

(**WINNIE-THE-POOH, pages 93–94**)

Kanga could escape by Jumping.

(**WINNIE-THE-POOH, page 118**)

'Well,' said Roo, 'can [Tiggers] jump as far as Kangas?'

'Yes,' said Tigger. 'When they want to.'

'I *love* jumping,' said Roo. 'Let's see who can

jump farthest, you or me.'

'*I* can,' said Tigger. 'But we mustn't stop now, or we shall be late.'

'Late for what?'

'For whatever we want to be in time for,' said Tigger, hurrying on.

(THE HOUSE AT POOH CORNER, pages 59–60)

See Also: **Anxiety; Anxious; Blinch; Escape;** *and* **Pluck.**

Jumping Animals, *Refer:* Jump.

Kk

Knight, *Refer:* **Sir Pooh De Bear, Knight.**

Knowledge, *abstract noun:* What you are after when instigorating. *Refer:* **Instigorate.**

Know Things, *Refer:* **Brain.**

Ll

Large Something, *phrasal noun*: Reward (edible).

'A Reward!' said Owl very loudly. 'We write a notice to say that we will give a large something to anybody who finds Eeyore's tail.'

'I see, I see,' said Pooh, nodding his head. 'Talking about large somethings,' he went on dreamily, 'I generally have a small something about now – about this time in the morning,' and he looked wistfully at the cupboard in the corner of Owl's parlour.

(**Winnie-the-Pooh,** **pages 46**)

Compare: **Little Something (to Revive One-Self).**

Late and Early, *proper names:* Inarticulate souls who say it all in the best way possible.

> Late and Early, two other friends-and-relations, said, 'Well, Early?' and 'Well, Late?' to each other in such a hopeless sort of way that it really didn't seem any good waiting for the answer.
>
> **(THE HOUSE AT POOH CORNER, pages 159–60)**

See Also: **Friends-And-Relations.**

Learn in Books, *verb:* To read, but it should be noted that Reading and Cleverness are not the same thing; in fact, that is why Readers lacking in Cleverness have to learn from books.

> [Piglet thought to himself] . . . . 'There's Rabbit. He hasn't Learnt in Books, but he can always Think of a Clever Plan.'
>
> **(WINNIE-THE-POOH, page 118)**

See Also: **Clever Reader; Educated;** *and* **Spelling.**

Learning, *noun* (although it looks like a *verb*): Interchangeable term with *Education,* but, more specially, the thing Rabbit knows as Education.
Refer: **A;** *and* **Educated.**

Listening-to-Me-Humming, *phrasal noun* (*from the verb* **to listen-to-me-humming-my-hums-to-you**): That nice sensation that pervades one's whole soul as an audience politely (better: enthusiastically) listens to one's nearest and dearest hums and poems.

> 'If I know anything about anything, that hole means Rabbit,' [Pooh] said, 'and Rabbit means Company,' he said, 'and Company means Food and Listening-to-Me-Humming and such like. *Rum-tum-tum-tiddle-um.*'
> **(WINNIE-THE-POOH, page 21)**

See Also: **Hum.**

Little Bit Extra, *phrasal noun*: The really important bits of one's anatomy that others have no regard for.

> Eeyore took his tail out of the water, and swished it from side to side.
> 'As I expected,' he said. 'Lost all feeling.

Numbed it. That's what it's done. Numbed it. Well, as long as nobody minds, I suppose it's all right.'

'Poor old Eeyore! I'll dry it for you,' said Christopher Robin, and he took out his handkerchief and rubbed it up.

'Thank you, Christopher Robin. You're the only one who seems to understand about tails.

They don't think – that's what's the matter with some of these others. They've no imagination. A tail isn't a tail to *them*, it's just a Little Bit Extra at the back.'

(WINNIE-THE-POOH, pages 113– 115)

Little Something (to Revive Oneself), *phrasal noun*: Any small amount of **Food***, especially if used to bolster and promote your absolute joy in life (and the bits you can freely eat of it).

Then they all went home again . . . . Roo had a hot bath and went straight to bed. But Pooh went back to his own house, and feeling very proud of what he had done, had a little something to revive himself.

(WINNIE-THE-POOH, page 116)

Long Start, *phrasal noun*: A Start that you do a long time before *someone else* bothers to get started (especially if she not only runs fast but is also really annoyed at you, and it is very Uncertain as to what she will do to you once she Catches Up).

PLAN TO CAPTURE BABY ROO

1. *General Remarks.* Kanga runs faster than any of Us, even Me (Rabbit).

2. *More General Remarks.* Kanga never takes her eye off Baby Roo, except when he's safely buttoned up in her pocket.

3. *Therefore.* If we are to capture Baby Roo, we must get a Long Start, because Kanga runs faster than any of Us, even Me. (*See* 1.)

(WINNIE-THE-POOH, page 85–86)

See Also: **Afterwards.**

Long Words, *adjective plus plural noun*:
Refer: **Encyclopaedia; Interesting Anecdote; Very Great Danger;** *and, since it is the longest word in this* **Dictionary, Worraworraworra-worraworra.**

Lost, *adjective*: **1** misplaced. **2** Impolitely Disappeared Without a Forwarding Address.

[Small] had been staying with Christopher Robin for a few seconds, and he started round a gorse-bush for exercise, but instead of coming back the other way, as expected, he hadn't, so nobody knew where he was.

'I expect he's just gone home,' said Christopher Robin to Rabbit . . . .

'Ha!' said Rabbit. After thinking a little, he went on:

'Has he written a letter saying how much he enjoyed himself, and how sorry he was he had to go so suddenly?'

Christopher Robin didn't think he had.

'Ha!' said Rabbit again, and looked very important. 'This is Serious. He is Lost.'

(THE HOUSE AT POOH CORNER, pages 45–46)

See Also: **Good-Bye-And-Thank-You-For-A-Nice-Time;** *and* **Scerching.**

Loud Noise (Making Such Until Rescued),

verb: What Eeyore would do in an **Anxious*** situation, and thus heartily recommended as the only thing to do in an Anxious situation. Indeed, you owe it to other animals.

What is the purpose of your suffering if not so others can learn from it?

'Eeyore could Escape by – by Making a Loud Noise Until Rescued.'
(WINNIE-THE-POOH, page 118)

Loud Sounds, *phrasal noun*: Specifically and generally, the nonsense other people make, especially when you are giving an excellent and interesting speech.

Eeyore coughed in an impressive way and began to speak . . . .
'What's Eeyore talking about?' Piglet whispered to Pooh.
'I don't know,' said Pooh rather dolefully.
'I thought it was *your* party.'
'I thought it was *once*. But I suppose it isn't.'
'I'd sooner it was yours than Eeyore's,' said Piglet.
'So would I,' said Pooh.
'H-hup!' said Roo again.
'AS – I – WAS – SAYING,' said Eeyore loudly and sternly, 'as I was saying when I was interrupted by various Loud Sounds.'
(WINNIE-THE-POOH, pages 142-43)

See Also: **Etceteras; Oddments;** *and* **Whatnots**.

Lumping, *verb*: What Heffalumps do, but without noticing anything.

> 'I saw a Heffalump to-day, Piglet.'
> 'What was it doing?' asked Piglet.
> 'Just lumping along,' said Christopher Robin. 'I don't think it saw *me*.'
> **(WINNIE-THE-POOH, page 51)**

Refer: **Heffalumping.**

Luncheon Time, *very important phrasal noun*: That time by which one should have eaten, shortly after a **Little Something (to Revive Oneself)*** at **Eleven O'clock***, and which should occur at **Home*** so you can rest afterward, or come back for seconds (before or after a little rest).

> 'Anyhow,' [Pooh] said, 'it is nearly Luncheon Time.'
> So he went home for it.
> **(WINNIE-THE-POOH, page 38)**

Mm

Mastershalums, *noun*: Actually, the flower nasturtium (genus *Nasturtium*), but this is how the name sounds if you have overfilled your mouth with honey and are busy softening it all up with your teeth.

> 'Besides, Pooh, it's a very difficult thing, planting, unless you know how to do it,' Piglet said . . . .
> 'I do know,' said Pooh, 'because Christopher Robin gave me a mastershalum seed, and I planted it, and I'm going to have mastershalums all over the front door.'
> 'I thought they were called nasturtiums,' said Piglet timidly . . . .
> 'No,' said Pooh. 'Not these. These are called mastershalums.'

(THE HOUSE AT POOH CORNER, pages 57–58)

Mean Anything, *phrasal noun*: Signify something.

Christopher Robin and Eeyore came strolling along together.

'I shouldn't be surprised if it hailed a good deal tomorrow,' Eeyore was saying. 'Blizzards and what-not. Being fine today doesn't Mean Anything. It has no sig – what's that word? Well, it has none of that. It's just a small piece of weather.'

'There's Pooh!' said Christopher Robin, who didn't much mind *what* it did tomorrow, as long as he was out in it.

'Hallo, Pooh!'

(THE HOUSE AT POOH CORNER, page 65)

See Also: **How; Inasmuch As Which.**

Medicine, *noun*: **1** extract of Malt, which is a nonfood item eaten for the sole purpose of increasing, in some way, your Strength or Size (as if something is wrong with your Size as it is!). **2** some animals (well, Tiggers, to be exact) have Extract of Malt as their **Food*** and call it *Strengthening* Medicine. It is well known that Malt-based Products, preferably in liquid form and in Larger Amounts, do make one feel quite braced and strengthened. However, the medicinal qualities of such are debatable.

'Now,' said Kanga, 'there's your medicine, and then bed.'

'W-w-what medicine?' said Piglet.

'To make you grow big and strong, dear. You don't want to grow up small and weak like Piglet, do you? Well, then!'

(WINNIE-THE-POOH, pages 95–96)

But Kanga and Christopher Robin and Piglet were all standing round Roo, watching him have his Extract of Malt. And Roo was saying, 'Must I?' and Kanga was saying, 'Now,

Roo dear, you remember what you promised.'

'What is it?' whispered Tigger to Piglet.

'His Strengthening Medicine,' said Piglet. 'He hates it.'

So Tigger came closer, and he leant over the back of Roo's chair, and suddenly he put out his tongue, and took one large golollop, and, with a sudden jump of surprise, Kanga said, 'Oh!' and then clutched at the spoon again just as it was disappearing, and pulled it safely back out of Tigger's mouth. But the Extract of Malt had gone . . .

Then Tigger looked up at the ceiling, and closed his eyes, and his tongue went round and round his chops, in case he had left any outside, and a peaceful smile came over his face as he said, 'So *that's* what Tiggers like!'

(**THE HOUSE AT POOH CORNER, pages 32–33**)

See Also: **Rapidity (Astonishing); Size (Favourite);** *and* **Strange Animal.**

Merest Accident, *phrasal noun*: As opposed to a **Hearty Joke***.

Missage, *noun*: An incomprehensible note that you misinterpret because (1) you assume the note *must* be for you and thus you bend its meaning to suit your predicament, or (2) you assume the note *must* be for you and yet you readily admit you can't read it, but that doesn't stop you from acting upon it.

And it was on the morning of the fourth day that Piglet's bottle came floating past him, and with one loud cry of 'Honey!' Pooh plunged into the water, seized the bottle, and struggled back to his tree again.

'Bother!' said Pooh, as he opened it. 'All that wet for nothing. What's that bit of paper doing?'

He took it out and looked.

'It's a Missage,' he said to himself, 'that's what it is. And that letter is a "P," and so is that, and so is that, and "P" means "Pooh," so it's a very important Missage to me, and I can't read it.'

(WINNIE-THE-POOH, page 123)

136

Compare: **Mysterious Missage.**

Mole, *noun:* Same as a **Pole*** but spelt differently.

> [Pooh said,] 'And we're going to discover a Pole
> or something. Or was it a Mole? Anyhow we're
> going to discover it.'
> **(WINNIE-THE-POOH, page 103)**

Moping (About), *verb:* Being **Gloomy*** because you have lost something of personal value *and* the world refuses to stop and sympathize. Although if you engage in moping about for long enough someone might stop and sympathize, and then you can get Sulky instead. Either way, it passes the time until **Tea*.**

> 'Hallo, Pooh,' [Owl] said. 'How's things?'
> 'Terrible and Sad,' said Pooh, 'because

Eeyore, who is a friend of mine, has lost his tail. And he's Moping about it. So could you very kindly tell me how to find it for him?'

(**Winnie-the-Pooh, page 45**)

Motherly, *adjective*: Just like a mother, aware of everything that happens (from missing vests to missing soap), and all that should happen (like eating watercress sandwiches), and everything you would rather forget (like missing soap and arithmetic), but is, despite all these faults, concerned about your safety in the Big Wide World.

Now it happened that Kanga had felt rather motherly that morning, and Wanting to Count Things – like Roo's vests, and how many pieces of soap there were left, and the two clean spots in Tigger's feeder; so she had sent them out with a packet of watercress sandwiches for Roo and a packet of extract-of-malt sandwiches for Tigger, to have a nice long morning in the Forest not getting into mischief.

(THE HOUSE AT POOH CORNER, pages 58–59)

Refer: **Affectionate Disposition; Anxious** *and, possibly,* **Fiercer Animal, Deprived of Its Young.**

Mysterious Missage, *phrasal noun:* A notice writen by someone who assumes that everyone else must know and understand what one says (and writes) because one thought it.

Pooh had wandered into the Hundred Acre Wood, and was standing in front of what had once been Owl's House. It didn't look at all like a house now; it looked like a tree which had

been blown down; as soon as a house looks like that, it is time you tried to find another one. Pooh had had a Mysterious Missage underneath his front door that morning, saying, 'I AM SCERCHING FOR A NEW HOUSE FOR OWL SO HAD YOU RABBIT,' and while he was wondering what it meant, Rabbit had come in and read it for him.

(THE HOUSE AT POOH CORNER, page 143)

Compare: **Missage**
See Also: **Clever Reader.**

Nn

Necessary Dorsal Muscles, *phrasal noun*: Certain muscles (the dorsal ones – the ones on your back) that you must have in order to fly (at all). The question of why the dorsal muscles specifically and not other types of muscles are necessary is a rather complicated problem, and some animals – well, a *particular* animal who does fly a lot – has been known to go through explaining it all so as to avoid physically difficult tasks.

'Could you fly up to the letter-box with Piglet on your back?' [Pooh] asked Owl.

'No,' said Piglet quickly. 'He couldn't.'

Owl explained about the Necessary Dorsal Muscles. He had explained this to Pooh and Christopher Robin once before, and had been waiting ever since for a

141

chance to do it again, because it is a thing which you can easily explain twice before anybody knows what you are talking about.

(THE HOUSE AT POOH CORNER, page 137)

See Also: **Fly; Interesting Anecdote;** *and* **Rhododendron.**

Noble Thing, *noun*: That act which is most Beneficial and Pleasing to another animal (but in no way could be described as a **Best Thing*** or even a **Good Thing*** for yourself). Noble Things usually involve allowing other animals of Unknown Eating and Cleaning Habits to reside in your **Home***.

'I have been told – the news has worked through to my corner of the Forest – the damp bit down on the right which nobody wants – that a certain Person is looking for a house. I have found one for him.' . . . .

So, in a little while, they came to the house which Eeyore had found . . . .

'There!' said Eeyore proudly, stopping them outside Piglet's house. 'And the name on it, and everything!'

'Oh!' cried Christopher Robin, wondering whether to laugh or what.

'Just the house for Owl. Don't you think so, little Piglet?'

And then Piglet did a Noble Thing, and he did it in a sort of dream, while he was thinking of all the wonderful words Pooh had hummed about him.

'Yes, it's just the house for Owl,' he said grandly. 'And I hope he'll be very happy in it.' And then he gulped twice, because he had been very happy in it himself.

(THE HOUSE AT POOH CORNER, pages 154–57)

Nobody, *noun*: **1** an animal so irked by company that he would deny his own existence and live in dark holes. **2** any animal who fails to recognize your intrinsic attractiveness and animality, and so fails to invite you in for **Tea***.

[Pooh] bent down, put his head into the hole, and called out:

'Is anybody at home?'

There was a sudden scuffling noise from

inside the hole, and then silence.

'What I said was, "Is anybody at home?"' called out Pooh very loudly.

'No!' said the voice; and then added, 'you needn't shout so loud. I heard you quite well the first time.'

'Bother!' said Pooh. 'Isn't there anybody here at all?'

'Nobody.'

(**Winnie-the-Pooh, page 21**)

See Also: **Rabbit.**

No Brain, *phrasal noun*: **Foolish and Deluded*,** but then that's an Admirable Quality in a Bear.

'Yes,' said Winnie-the-Pooh.
'I see now,' said Winnie-the-Pooh.

'I have been Foolish and Deluded,' said he, 'and I am a Bear of No Brain at All.'

'You're the Best Bear in All the World,' said Christopher Robin soothingly.

'Am I?' said Pooh hopefully. And then he brightened up suddenly.

(**WINNIE-THE-POOH, page 38**)

See Also: **Brain; Positively Startling Lack of Brain;** *and* **Very Little Brain.**

No Exchange of Thought, *phrasal noun*:

When no one talks to you.

'Nobody tells me,' said Eeyore. 'Nobody keeps me Informed. I make it seventeen days come Friday since anybody spoke to me.'

. . . . 'And today's Saturday,' said Rabbit. 'So that would make it eleven days. And I was here myself a week ago.'

'Not conversing,' said Eeyore. 'Not first one and then the other. You said "Hallo" and Flashed Past. I saw your tail in the distance as I was meditating my reply. I *had* thought of saying "What?" – but, of course, it was then too late.'

'Well, I was in a hurry.'

'No Give and Take,' Eeyore went on. 'No Exchange of Thought. "*Hallo – What*" – I mean, it gets you nowhere, particularly if the other person's tail is only just in sight for the second half of the conversation.'

(The House At Pooh Corner, page 147)

No Give and Take, *Refer:* No Exchange of Thought.

North Pole, *phrasal noun:* Literally, 'the thing you discover,' despite not knowing what it is you're discovering, nor where it might be.

146

'Oh!' said Pooh again. 'What *is* the North Pole?' he asked.

'It's just a thing you discover,' said Christopher Robin carelessly, not being quite sure himself.

'Oh! I see,' said Pooh. 'Are bears any good at discovering it?'

'Of course they are.'

(WINNIE-THE-POOH, pages 101–02)

As soon as he had finished his lunch Christopher Robin whispered to Rabbit, and Rabbit said, 'Yes, yes, of course,' and they walked a little way up the stream together.

'I didn't want the others to hear,' said Christopher Robin.

'Quite so,' said Rabbit, looking important.

'It's – I wondered – It's only – Rabbit, I suppose *you* don't know, What does the North Pole *look* like.'

'Well,' said Rabbit, stroking his whiskers, 'now you're asking me.'

'I did know once, only I've sort of forgotten,' said Christopher Robin carelessly.

'It's a funny thing,' said Rabbit, 'but I've sort of forgotten too, although I did know *once*.'

'I suppose it's just a pole stuck in the ground?'

'Sure to be a pole,' said Rabbit, 'because of

calling it a pole, and if it's a pole, well, I should think it would be sticking in the ground, shouldn't you, because there'd be nowhere else to stick it.'

'Yes, that's what I thought.'

'The only thing,' said Rabbit, 'is, *where is it sticking?*'

'That's what we're looking for,' said Christopher Robin.

(WINNIE-THE-POOH, pages 109–110)

See Also: **Mole.**

Nothing, *noun:* Does *not* mean 'Not a Thing,' but refers to the Very Best Thing in All the World: a state of relaxation and peace – just you and thou and a smackerel or two, and no one bothering.

'I like that too,' said Christopher Robin, 'but what I like *doing* best is Nothing.'

'How do you do Nothing?' asked Pooh, after he had wondered for a long time.

'Well, it's when people call out at you just as you're going off to do it, What are you going to do, Christopher Robin, and you say, Oh, nothing, and then you go and do it.'

'Oh, I see,' said Pooh.

'This is a nothing sort of thing that we're doing now.'

'Oh, I see,' said Pooh again.

'It means just going along, listening to all the things you can't hear, and not bothering.'

'Oh!' said Pooh.

(THE HOUSE AT POOH CORNER, page 169)

IMMEDIATELY REFER BACK TO: BEST THING.

No Wonder, *exclamation*: Shortened form of the simple statement 'Everything is explained and accounted for, and no further discussion or thought need be given to the matter at hand, as it all really is so apparently obvious.'

'That Accounts for a Good Deal,' said Eeyore gloomily. 'It Explains Everything. No Wonder.'

(**Winnie-the-Pooh, page 42**)

See Also: **It Explains Everything.**

Oo

Oddments, *noun*: Those animals who seem to live in the Forest but are not necessarily your friends. Which isn't to say these animals *aren't* Friendly but are rather *just* present.

> Eeyore coughed in an impressive way and began to speak.
> 'Friends,' he said, 'including oddments, it is a great pleasure, or perhaps I had better say it has been a pleasure so far, to see you at my party.'
>
> (**WINNIE-THE-POOH**, page 142)

See Also: **Etceteras; Friends-And-Relations;** *and* **What-Nots.**

Old Grey Donkey: Eeyore.

Organdized, to Be, *verb*: Told What to Do, which you shall be, sooner or later, by Someone Else. Being organdized requires one of two responses. First, smaller animals should agree and quietly disappear home. Or, second, larger animals should agree and absent themselves. Either way, just nod your head and leave those in charge to be, well, *charging*.

> 'Now,' said Rabbit, 'this is a Search, and I've Organized it –'
> 'Done what to it?' said Pooh.
> 'Organized it. Which means – well, it's what you do to a Search, when you don't all look in the same place at once. So I want *you,* Pooh, to search by the Six Pine Trees first, and then work your way towards Owl's House, and look out for me there. Do you see?'
> 'No,' said Pooh. 'What –'
> 'Then I'll see you at Owl's House in about an hour's time.'
> 'Is Piglet organdized too?'
> 'We all are,' said Rabbit, and off he went.

(THE HOUSE AT POOH CORNER, page 37)

See Also: **Bath; Captainish;** *and* **Washing Nonsense (Behind The Ears).**

Out of All Danger, to Be, *phrasal verb*: To be safely protected by the Presence of a Larger Animal of Friendly Intent.

> 'It's Christopher Robin,' Pooh said.
> 'Ah, then you'll be all right,' said Piglet.
> 'You'll be quite safe with *him*. Good-bye,' and he trotted off home as quickly as he could, very glad to be Out of All Danger again.
>
> **(WINNIE-THE-POOH, page 36)**

P.D., *abbreviation:* **Pole Discoverer*.**
Refer: **Winnie-The-Pooh, Honorific Titles Thereof.**

Plan, *Refer:* **Learn in Books;** and **Very Clever Pup-Pup-Pup Plan.**

Ples, *verb* (short for 'May it please you to'): Owl's rendition of *please*.

> Owl lived at The Chestnuts . . . . Underneath the knocker there was a notice which said:
> PLES RING IF AN RNSER IS REQUIRD.
>> **(WINNIE-THE-POOH, page 43)**

See Also: **Clever Reader; Plez; Rnser/Rnsr;** *and* **Spelling**.

Plez, *verb*: Owl's version of **Ples***.

     Underneath the bell-pull there was a notice which said:
     Plez Cnoke if an Rnsr is Not Reqid.
          (**Winnie-the-Pooh, page 43**)

See Also: **Clever Reader; Ples; Rnser/Rnsr;** *and* **Spelling.**

Pluck, *noun*: Bravery; a certain lack of **Blinch***.

     'Piglet,' said Rabbit, taking out a pencil, and licking the end of it, 'you haven't any pluck.'
     'It is hard to be brave,' said Piglet, sniffing slightly, 'when you're only a Very Small Animal.'
          (**Winnie-the-Pooh, page 84**)

Poem, *noun:* **1** Eeyore's one and only poem. **2** hence, any singular achievement.

> [Eeyore] coughed in an important way, and began again . . . . 'I have a piece of Poetry to read to you. Hitherto – hitherto – a long word meaning – well, you'll see what it means directly – hitherto, as I was saying, all the Poetry in the Forest has been written by Pooh, a Bear with a Pleasing Manner but a Positively Startling Lack of Brain. The Poem which I am now about to read to you was written by Eeyore, or Myself, in a Quiet Moment. If somebody will take Roo's bull's-eye away from him, and wake up Owl, we shall all be able to enjoy it. I call it – POEM.'

(THE HOUSE AT POOH CORNER, pages 161–62)

See Also: **Hum;** *and* **Singy.**

Poetry, *Refer:* **Hum.**

Pole, *noun*: Any Object of Uncertain Place, Quality, or Lasting Benefit that is still worth discovering, especially First (Before Anyone Else). (Just in case.)

Pooh couldn't answer that one, so he began to sing.

They all went off to discover the Pole,
    Owl and Piglet and Rabbit and all;
It's a Thing you Discover, as I've been tole
    By Owl and Piglet and Rabbit and all.
                        (WINNIE-THE-POOH, page 106)

See Also: **Expedition; Expotition; Mole; North Pole;** *and* **Poles (Other).**

Pole Discoverer, same as **P.D.*** *Refer:* **Winnie-The-Pooh, Honorific Titles Thereof.**

Poles (Other), *noun*: While the **North Pole***
is something you discover, the South, East, and West
Poles are somethings you would rather not discover
(and if you did, it is best not to talk about it, and
certainly you'll eat better if you forget about it).

> 'There's a South Pole,' said Christopher
> Robin, 'and I expect there's an East Pole and a
> West Pole, though people don't like talking
> about them.'
> Pooh was very excited when he heard this,
> and suggested that they should have an
> Expotition to discover the East Pole, but
> Christopher Robin had thought of something
> else to do with Kanga; so Pooh went out to
> discover the East Pole by himself. Whether he
> discovered it or not, I forget.
>
> **(WINNIE-THE-POOH, page 121)**

Refer: **East Pole.**
See Also: **Expedition**; *and* **Expotition**.

PooH, *signature*: Pooh's signature:

Poohing, *active verb*: A poetic expression celebrating Pooh's intrinsic bear-ness.

> *That the summer, which is coming,*
> *Will be fun.*
> *And the cows are almost cooing,*
> *And the turtle-doves are mooing,*
> *Which is why a Pooh is poohing*
> *In the sun.*

(from *NOISE, BY POOH*)
(THE HOUSE AT POOH CORNER, page 79)

Refer: **Hum**.

Poohsticks, *noun*: A very simple game requiring Players, Sticks, a Bridge, and a Flowing River (under the Bridge – this is very important). The object of the game is, having dropped the sticks over the side of the bridge that faces *from where* the river comes, to have the sticks race under

the bridge. (You know which is your stick by marking it.) Having dropped the stick, you run to the other side of the bridge (the side facing *to where* the river is going) to see which stick comes out first. Simple. The game was discovered and developed by the poet Pooh, but nonetheless requires some skill, and winning all depends on how expertly you handle the dropping bit of the game.

He had just come to the bridge; and not looking where he was going, he tripped over something, and the fir-cone jerked out of his paw into the river.

'Bother,' said Pooh, as it floated slowly under the bridge, and he went back to get another fir-cone which had a rhyme to it. But then he thought that he would just look at the river instead, because it was a peaceful sort of day, so he lay down and looked at it, and it slipped slowly away beneath him . . . and suddenly, there was his fir-cone slipping away too.

'That's funny,' said Pooh. 'I dropped it on the other side,' said Pooh, 'and it came out on this side! I wonder if it would do it again?' And he went back for some more fir-cones.

It did. It kept on doing it. Then he dropped two in at once, and leant over the bridge to see which of them would come out first; and one of

them did; but as they were both the same size, he didn't know if it was the one which he wanted to win, or the other one. So the next time he dropped one big one and one little one, and the big one came out first, which was what he had said it would do, and the little one came out last, which was what he had said it would do, so he had won twice ... and when he went home for tea, he had won thirty-six and lost twenty-eight, which meant that he was – that he had – well, you take twenty-eight from thirty-six, and *that's* what he was. Instead of the other way round.

And that was the beginning of the game called Poohsticks, which Pooh invented, and which he and his friends used to play on the edge of the Forest. But they played with sticks instead of fir-cones, because they were easier to mark.

(THE HOUSE AT POOH CORNER, pages 91–92)

'I think we all ought to play Poohsticks,' [said Christopher Robin.]

So they did. And Eeyore, who had never played it before, won more times than anybody else; and Roo fell in twice, the first time by accident and the second time on purpose, because he suddenly saw Kanga coming from the Forest, and he knew he'd have to go to bed anyhow. So then Rabbit said he'd go with them; and Tigger and Eeyore went off together, because Eeyore wanted to tell Tigger How to Win at Poohsticks, which you do by letting your stick drop in a twitchy sort of way, if you understand what I mean, Tigger.

(THE HOUSE AT POOH CORNER, pages 104–05)

Pooh Trap for Heffalumps, *Refer:* Cunning Trap; Heffalump Trap (For Poohs); *and* Very Deep Pit.

Poohanpiglet Corner, *phrasal noun*: From the fact that Poohanpiglet Corner could have referred to a particular part of the Forest, it is a phrase that can be used to express the regret that something could have been, if something else didn't sound better.

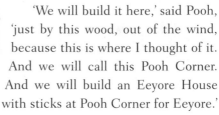

'We will build it here,' said Pooh, 'just by this wood, out of the wind, because this is where I thought of it. And we will call this Pooh Corner. And we will build an Eeyore House with sticks at Pooh Corner for Eeyore.'

'There was a heap of sticks on the other side of the wood,' said Piglet. 'I saw them. Lots and lots. All piled up.'

'Thank you, Piglet,' said Pooh. 'What you have just said will be a Great Help to us, and because of it I could call this place Poohanpiglet Corner if Pooh Corner didn't sound better, which it does, being smaller and more like a corner. Come along.'

(THE HOUSE AT POOH CORNER, pages 7–8)

See Also: **Awful Mistake.**

Pootel, *noun*: A name bestowed upon Piglet after he was stripped of his dignity by being forced to wash. And having been stripped of his dignity, he was discussed as a thing instead of a brave, gallant, and deeply intelligent Piglet (which he is!).

'There you are!' said Piglet. 'I told you so. I'm Piglet.'

Christopher Robin shook his head again.

'Oh, you're not Piglet,' he said. 'I know

Piglet well, and he's *quite* a different colour.'

Piglet began to say that this was because he had just had a bath . . . .

'I knew it wasn't Piglet,' said Kanga. 'I wonder who it can be.'

'Perhaps it's some relation of Pooh's,' said Christopher Robin. 'What about a nephew or an uncle or something?'

Kanga agreed that this was probably what it was, and said that they would have to call it by some name.

'I shall call it Pootel,' said Christopher Robin. 'Henry Pootel for short.'

And just when it was decided, Henry Pootel wriggled out of Kanga's arms and jumped to the ground. To his great joy Christopher Robin had left the door open. Never had Henry Pootel Piglet run so fast as he ran then.

(**WINNIE-THE-POOH, page 97**)

See Also: **Bath;** *perhaps* **Washing Nonsense (Behind The Ears);** *and, certainly,* **Hearty joke.**

Positively Startling Lack of Brain, *long phrasal noun*: A compliment of high praise given to a poet, that is, to someone of **Very Little Brain***.

> 'Hitherto – hitherto – a long word meaning – well, you'll see what it means directly – hitherto, as I was saying, all the Poetry in the Forest has been written by Pooh, a Bear with a Pleasing Manner but a Positively Startling Lack of Brain,' [said Eeyore.]
> **(THE HOUSE AT POOH CORNER, page 162)**

Po-things, *same as*: PROVISIONS (but easier to say).

Problem of Escape, *Refer*: **Escape.**

Proper Tea, *Refer*: **Tea.**

Provisions/Po-things, *noun* (either spelling will do): **1** specifically, Things to Eat while on an **Expedition***. **2** hence, what **Food*** there is when you are not at **Home***.

> 'It's an Expedition,' [said Christopher Robin] . . . . 'And we must all bring Provisions.'
> 'Bring what?'
> 'Things to eat.'
> 'Oh!' said Pooh happily. 'I thought you said Provisions. I'll go and tell them.' And he

stumped off.

The first person he met was Rabbit . . . .

'Yes. And we're going to discover a Pole or something . . . . '

'We are, are we?' said Rabbit.

'Yes. And we've got to bring Po-things to eat with us. In case we want to eat them. Now I'm going down to Piglet's. Tell Kanga, will you?'

(**WINNIE-THE-POOH**, pages 102–03)

Qq

Quiet and Refined, *phrasal adjective:* **1** what one becomes after a good breakfast (or any meal, for that matter). **2** Full and Replete.

And Tigger, who had been hiding behind trees and jumping out on Pooh's shadow when it wasn't looking, said that Tiggers were only bouncy before breakfast, and that as soon as they had had a few haycorns they became Quiet and Refined.

(THE HOUSE AT POOH CORNER, page 23)

R r

Rabbit, *verb* (*from* the name of Rabbit): To assume an identity other than your own, often so as to make a Joke or to avoid meeting Others.

> 'Hallo, Rabbit, isn't that you?' said Pooh.
> 'No,' said Rabbit, in a different sort of voice this time.
> 'But isn't that Rabbit's voice?'
> 'I don't *think* so,' said Rabbit. 'It isn't *meant* to be.'
> 'Oh!' said Pooh.
> **(WINNIE-THE-POOH, pages 21–22)**

The first person Pooh met was Rabbit.
'Hallo, Rabbit,' he said, 'is that you?'

'Let's pretend it isn't,' said Rabbit, 'and see what happens.'

'I've got a message for you.'

'I'll give it to him.'

(**WINNIE-THE-POOH, page 102**)

See Also: **Hearty Joke; Nobody;** *and* **Sanders**.

Rabbit's Companion, *Refer:* Winnie-The-Pooh, Honorific Titles Thereof.

Rapidity (Astonishing), *noun:* Something that Tiggers have that keeps them full of **Bounce***. (Possibly this is something like **Medicine***, but no one is sure, not even Tiger.)

'I should hate him to go *on* being Sad,' said Piglet doubtfully.

'Tiggers never go on being Sad,' explained Rabbit. 'They get over it with Astonishing Rapidity. I asked Owl, just to make sure, and he said that that's what they always get over it with.'

(**THE HOUSE AT POOH CORNER, page 110**)

R.C., short form of **Rabbit's Companion***. *Refer*: **Winnie-The-Pooh, Honorific Titles Thereof.**

Reader, *noun*: By definition, a Reader is always a **Clever Reader***.

Ready for Anything, *phrasal adjective*: Prepared emotionally, psychologically, and mentally for whatever happens or not, especially if you have just eaten, and probably won't need to think of eating again for a little while. It is Useful to be so prepared at the start of an **Adventure***.

> Pooh knew that an Adventure was going to happen, and he brushed the honey off his nose with the back of his paw, and spruced himself ·up as well as he could, so as to look Ready for Anything.
>
> **(WINNIE-THE-POOH, page 100)**

See Also: **Big Boots;** *and* **Braces.**

Real Brain, *abstract noun*: A Dictionary that you have in your head so you don't have to know words or letters, but can just think a question and the Dictionary will tell you.

And Pooh, his back against one of the sixty-something trees, and his paws folded in front of him, said, 'Oh!' and 'I didn't know,' and thought how wonderful it would be to have a Real Brain which could tell you things.

(**THE HOUSE AT POOH CORNER**, page 172)

See Also: **Brain; Clever Reader;** *and* **Learn in Books.**

Remove Stiffness, *phrasal verb*: **Generally Regarded*,** it is a Necessary Thing to Do After Walking, and the calisthenics, stretching, or snoozing you do (after the walking bit) are how you do it. Although it could also refer to making the decision not to bother walking again, given the aches it causes.

So round this spinney went Pooh and Piglet after them, Piglet passing the time by telling Pooh what his Grandfather Trespassers W had done to Remove Stiffness after Tracking.

(WINNIE-THE-POOH, page 34)

See Also: **Shortness of Breath; Short Walk;** *and* **Thinking Walk.**

Reqid, *verb*: The emphatic form of *required,* used to indicate to the listener (or reader) that something is indeed NOT required.

Underneath the bell-pull there was a notice which said:

PLEZ CNOKE IF AN RNSR IS NOT REQID.

(WINNIE-THE-POOH, page 43)

See Also: **Requird;** *and* **Rnser/Rnsr.**

Reqird, *verb*: Alternative spelling of *required.* Simple.

Underneath the knocker there was a notice which said:

PLES RING IF AN RNSER IS REQIRD.

(WINNIE-THE-POOH, page 43)

See Also: **Rnser/Rnsr;** *and* **Spelling.**

Rescue is Coming, *exclamation, from the verb* TO RESCUE: A slogan used by Rescuers to ease and please Those in Need, especially if the Rescuers aren't sure what, how, or when they might Rescue (and what will happen after that).

'We must rescue [Piglet] at once! I thought he was with *you,* Pooh. Owl, could you rescue him on your back?' said Christopher Robin.

'I don't think so,' said Owl, after grave thought. 'It is doubtful if the necessary dorsal muscles –'

'Then would you fly to him at *once* and say that Rescue is Coming? And Pooh and I will think of a Rescue and come as quick as ever we can. Oh, don't *talk,* Owl, go on quick!' And, still thinking of something to say, Owl flew off.

(**WINNIE-THE-POOH**, page 128)

See Also: **Afterwards.**

Respect, *noun*: **1** admiration of someone who has **Spelling***. **2** admiration of a quality or ability in someone that is not necessarily important for everybody every time, but is worth a mention now and again.

'After all,' said Rabbit to himself, 'Christopher Robin depends on Me. He's fond of Pooh and Piglet and Eeyore, and so am I, but they haven't any Brain. Not to notice. And he respects Owl, because you can't help respecting anybody who can spell TUESDAY, even if he doesn't spell it right; but spelling isn't everything. There are days when spelling Tuesday simply doesn't count.'
     (**THE HOUSE AT POOH CORNER, page 73**)

Respectful Song, *phrasal noun*: **1** a Good Song (by Pooh) that was hummed to reward and celebrate Piglet's extreme **Pluck*** (and lack of **Blinch***) in doing a **Very Grand Thing***. **2** any Song that is more rewarding than the achievement it celebrates.

'It won't break,' whispered Pooh comfortingly, 'because you're a Small Animal, and I'll stand underneath, and if you save us all, it will be a Very Grand Thing to talk about afterwards, and perhaps I'll make up a Song, and people will say "It was so grand what Piglet did that a Respectful Pooh Song was made about it!"'

(THE HOUSE AT POOH CORNER, page 139)

See Also: **Hum**; *and* **Singy**.

Rhododendron, *noun*: A Useful Word to bring up in any Involved Conversation. R*efer*: **Interesting Anecdote**.

Right, *noun*: The thing or activity that invariably you didn't guess correctly the first time, but could the second time, especially if you had only two choices.

'I *think* it's more to the right,' said Piglet nervously. 'What do *you* think, Pooh?'

Pooh looked at his two paws. He knew that one of them was the right, and he knew that when you had decided which one of them was the right, then the other one was the left, but he never could remember how to begin.

'Well,' he said slowly.

(THE HOUSE AT POOH CORNER, page 116)

Rissolution, *noun*: A decision made by any **Captainish*** sort of animal, who can write it up (more or less) in notice form, which must have at least three aspects:

1. It is brief.
2. It took a long time to write up.
3. It is difficult to understand.
4. It is assumed you will agree with it (and you will if you know what is good for you).

One day when he felt that he couldn't wait any longer, Rabbit brained out a Notice, and this is what it said:

'Notice a meeting of everybody will meet at the House at Pooh Corner to pass a Rissolution By Order Keep to the Left Signed Rabbit.'

He had to write this out two or three times before he could get the rissolution to look like what he thought it was going to when he began to spell it: but, when at last it was finished, he took it round to everybody and read it out to them. And they all said they would come.

(THE HOUSE AT POOH CORNER, page 160)

177

See Also: **Mysterious Missage;** *and* **Spelling.**

Rnser/Rnsr, *very bad spelling*: Answer. *Refer:* **Ples; Plez; Reqid; Reqird;** *and* **Respect.**

Roo-Noise, *noun*: Polite expression for the bodily expression of digestive enjoyment of whatever it was you consumed earlier that day. So called after the obvious noises Baby Roo must make.

> Piglet made a squeaky Roo-noise from the bottom of Kanga's pocket.
> **(WINNIE-THE-POOH, page 91)**

Refer: **Ee-ers O I A-ors.**

Ss

Sadness and Despair, *phrasal noun:* What you experience that very instant when you realize that all one's hopes and aspirations, joys and triumphs mean nothing, because you've just gone and done a deeply embarrassing and foolish act and there is no way to undo it. And only one thing seems even worse: doing the Pluckish thing of Taking the Consequences.

And all the time Winnie-the-Pooh had been trying to get the honey-jar off his head. The more he shook it, the more tightly it stuck. *'Bother!'* he said, inside the jar, and *'Oh! Help!'* and, mostly, *'Ow!'* And he tried bumping it against things, but as he couldn't see what he was bumping it against, it didn't help him; and he tried to climb out of the Trap, but as he could see nothing but jar, and not much of that, he couldn't find his way. So at last he lifted up his head, jar and all, and made a loud, roaring noise of Sadness and Despair.

(WINNIE-THE-POOH, page 62)

Compare: **Gloomy.**

Sanders, *nom de guerre:* The assumed name under which Pooh plays, eats, and snoozes, as opposed to his *nom de plume,* the assumed name under which he writes (that is, **PooH***). Either way, Pooh is Pooh, or Edward Bear, or Winnie-the-Pooh, or even **Sir Pooh de Bear, Knight*.**

Winnie-the-Pooh lived in a forest all by himself under the name of Sanders.

('What does "under the name" mean?' asked Christopher Robin.

'It means he had the name over the door in gold letters and lived under it.')

(WINNIE-THE-POOH, page 2)

See Also: **Winnie-The-Pooh, Honorific Titles Thereof.**

Scerching, *verb:* There is the possibility that this word is a misspelling of *searching* (but to say this would cast unreasonable doubts over Rabbit's Education and **Spelling***). More probable is that 'scerching' is a mixture of *searching for* and *scavenging for*. Hence, 'to scerch' is to be in pursuit of a something for free.

I AM SCERCHING FOR A NEW HOUSE
FOR OWL SO HAD YOU RABBIT.
(**The House At Pooh Corner**, page 147)

Seeing What Everybody Else Thought About It, *phrasal noun*: **1** to gossip. **2** to discuss with others the pressing issues of the day (such as who's doing what, why, and how).

It was going to be one of Rabbit's busy days. As soon as he woke up he felt important, as if everything depended upon him. It was just the day for Organizing Something, or for Writing a Notice Signed Rabbit, or for Seeing What Everybody Else Thought About It.

(**The House At Pooh Corner**, page 71)

Compare: **What-Shall-I-Do-About-You-Know-What.**

Serious, *adjective*: Pooh's way of saying 'Not Pleasant.'

> 'This is Serious,' said Pooh. 'I must have an Escape.'
> **(WINNIE-THE-POOH, page 122)**

See Also: **Escape;** *and* **Lost**.

Shortness of Breath, *phrasal noun*: A condition of old age in which you can't go for Walks in the open air any longer.

> So round this spinney went Pooh and Piglet after [the two Woozles], Piglet passing the time by telling Pooh . . . how his Grandfather Tresspassers W had suffered in his later years from Shortness of Breath, and other matters of interest.
> **(WINNIE-THE-POOH, page 34)**

See Also: **Grandfathers; Short Walk; Stoutness Exercises; Thinking Walk; Trespassers W;**

Trespassers Will; *and* **Trespassers William.**

Short Walk, *phrasal noun*: A walk that is brief, Friendly, and allows for plenty of fresh air. In fact, the purpose of Short Walks (as opposed to **Thinking Walks*** and **Jostles***) is to develop Breathing, given that as we all get older **Shortness of Breath*** can be a problem.

> Christopher Robin jumped up.
> 'Come on, Pooh,' he said.
> 'Come on, Tigger!' cried Roo.
> 'Shall we go, Owl?' said Rabbit . . . .
> Eeyore waved them back.
> 'Christopher Robin and I are going for a Short Walk,' he said, 'not a Jostle. If he likes to bring Pooh and Piglet with him, I shall be glad of their company, but one must be able to Breathe.'

(THE HOUSE AT POOH CORNER, pages 155–56)

Silly, *adjective*: A term of endearment that should be reserved for someone you love very much but whose brain capacity you doubt.

> 'Hallo, are you stuck?' he asked.
> 'N-no,' said Pooh carelessly. 'Just resting and thinking and humming to myself.'
> 'Here, give us a paw.'

Pooh Bear stretched out a paw, and Rabbit pulled and pulled and pulled . . .

'*Ow!*' cried Pooh. 'You're hurting!'

'The fact is,' said Rabbit, 'you're stuck . . . . Well, well, I shall go and fetch Christopher Robin.'

Christopher Robin lived at the other end of the Forest, and when he came back with Rabbit, and saw the front half of Pooh, he said, 'Silly old Bear,' in such a loving voice that everybody felt quite hopeful again.

(**Winnie-the-Pooh, pages 24–25**)

'Going on an Expotition?' said Pooh eagerly. 'I don't think I've ever been on one of those. Where are we going to on this Expotition?'

'Expedition, silly old Bear.'

(**Winnie-the-Pooh, page 101**)

See Also: **Affectionate Disposition.**

Singy, *adjective*: Happy. Very Happy. Really-Happy-and-I-Don't-Care-Because-I-Can-Hum Happy.

> One day, when Pooh was walking towards this bridge, he was trying to make up a piece of poetry about fir-cones, because there they were, lying about on each side of him, and he felt singy. So he picked a fir-cone up, and looked at it, and said to himself, 'This is a very good fir-cone, and something ought to rhyme to it.' But he couldn't think of anything.

(THE HOUSE AT POOH CORNER, pages 90–91)

See Also: **Hum.**

Sir Pooh De Bear, Knight, *titled personage*: An honorific title of Winnie-the-Pooh, one of many, which proves that being **Astute*** and having a **Positively Startling Lack of Brain*** is no hindrance to honor and glory, faithfulness, and polite behavior.

> 'Could a Bear be one?'
> 'Of course he could!' said Christopher Robin. 'I'll make you one.' And he took a stick and touched Pooh on the shoulder, and said, 'Rise, Sir Pooh de Bear, most faithful of all my Knights.'

So Pooh rose and sat down and said 'Thank you,' which is the proper thing to say when you have been made a Knight.

(THE HOUSE AT POOH CORNER, pages 173–74)

See Also: **Winnie-The-Pooh, Honorific Titles Thereof.**

Sitting on Thistles, *Refer:* Thought for Others.

Size, Favourite, *phrasal noun*: **1** specifically, the size of Piglet, which is Very Small and roundish, which is what both **Balloons*** and Piglets should be. **2** hence, generally, it refers to the size of anyone who fits that description and toward whom you feel rather favoured.

'Thank you, Piglet,' said Eeyore. 'You don't mind my asking,' he went on, 'but what colour was this balloon when it – when it *was* a balloon?'
'Red.'
'I just wondered . . . Red,' he murmured to himself. 'My favourite colour . . . How big was it?'
'About as big as me.'

'I just wondered . . . About as big as Piglet,' he said to himself sadly. 'My favourite size. Well, well.'

(WINNIE-THE-POOH, pages 78–79)

See Also: **Fond of Pigs.**

Skoos Ee, *polite verbal expression*: How one should properly say 'Excuse me' when one has a mouth full of food.

Refer: **Ee-ers O I A-ors.**

Smack, *noun*: That indefinable *thing* that is required to really make appreciation heartfelt, especially as expressed by Clapping.

'If anyone wants to clap,' said Eeyore when he had read this, 'now is the time to do it.'
They all clapped.
'Thank you,' said Eeyore. 'Unexpected and gratifying, if a little lacking in Smack.'

(THE HOUSE AT POOH CORNER, pages 163-64)

Smackerel, *noun*: Very like Smackerels, but unfortunately only one of them.

See Also: **Breakfast; Company; Condensed Milk; Eleven O'Clock; Extract of Malt; Food;**

Haycorns; Hunny; Large Something; Little Something (To Revive Oneself); Luncheon Time; Provisions/Po-Things; *and* **Tea.**

Small and Weak, *phrasal adjective*: **1** specifically, like the limited muscular and aerobic capability of Piglet. **2** hence, generally, any such limited physical ability. (Rather uncalled-for comparison, given that Piglet is nice, small, and roundish.)

'Now,' said Kanga, 'there's your medicine . . . . To make you grow big and strong, dear. You don't want to grow up small and weak like Piglet, do you? Well, then!'
(WINNIE-THE-POOH, pages 95–96)

Refer: Size, Favourite.

Smudge/The Smear, *abstract noun*: **1** how Baby Roo attempts to sign his name; that is, throw a painted paw at a piece of paper and call it done. **2** what remains of a Work of Art after it is mistaken for a piece of furniture.

'The rissolution,' said Rabbit, 'is that we all sign it, and take it to Christopher Robin.'
So it was signed . . . SMUDGE.
(THE HOUSE AT POOH CORNER, pages 164–65)

'I am calling it this,' said Owl importantly, and he showed them what he had been making. It was a square piece of board with the name of the house painted on it:

THE WOLERY

It was at this exciting moment that something came through the trees, and bumped into Owl. The board fell to the ground, and Piglet and Roo bent over it eagerly.

'Oh, it's you,' said Owl crossly.

'Hallo, Eeyore!' said Rabbit. '*There* you are! Where have *you* been?' Eeyore took no notice of them.

'Good morning, Christopher Robin,' he said, brushing away Roo and Piglet, and sitting down on THE WOLERY . . . .

Owl, who had just discovered that his new address was THE SMEAR, coughed at Eeyore sternly, but said nothing, and Eeyore, with most of THE WOLERY behind him, marched off with his friends.

(THE HOUSE AT POOH CORNER, pages 153–56)

Not to Be Confused With: SPUDGE.

189

Social Round, The, *phrasal noun*: Whatever it is everyone else is up to and you are never invited to join.

> 'I might have known,' said Eeyore. 'After all, one can't complain. I have my friends. Somebody spoke to me only yesterday. And was it last week or the week before that Rabbit bumped into me and said 'Bother!' The Social Round. Always something going on.'
> Nobody was listening.
> **(Winnie-the-Pooh, page 143)**

South Pole, *Refer*: **Poles (Other).**

Special Pencil Case, *phrasal noun*: A unique and superlative gift that you and no one else would appreciate or deserve.

> Nobody was listening, for they were all saying, 'Open it, Pooh,' 'What is it, Pooh?' 'I know what it is,' 'No, you don't,' and other helpful remarks of this sort. And of course Pooh was opening it as quickly as ever he could, but without cutting the string, because you never know when a bit of string might be Useful. At last it was undone.
> When Pooh saw what it was, he nearly fell down, he was so pleased. It was a Special

Pencil Case . . . which shut with a click when you clicked it.

(**Winnie-the-Pooh, pages 143–44**)

See Also: **B.**

Spelling, *noun:* The ability to read and write squiggles (that have certain meanings attached to them), and so tell other people things without having to explain to each and every one exactly what it is you think worth telling them. Obviously, some **Brain*** is required, but not much, since Piglet can read fairly well (and he has only **Fluff***).

These notices had been written by Christopher Robin, who was the only one in the forest who could spell; for Owl, wise though he was in many ways, able to read and write and spell his own name WOL, yet somehow went all to pieces over delicate words like MEASLES and BUTTEREDTOAST.

WOL

(**Winnie-the-Pooh, pages 43–44**)

'After all,' said Rabbit to himself, 'Christopher Robin depends on Me. He's fond of Pooh and Piglet and Eeyore, and so am I, but they haven't any Brain. Not to notice.

And he respects Owl, because you can't help respecting anybody who can spell TUESDAY, even if he doesn't spell it right; but spelling isn't everything. There are days when spelling Tuesday simply doesn't count.'

(THE HOUSE AT POOH CORNER, page 73)

See Also: **Clever Reader; Respect; Wobble;** *and, to keep a perspective on what is really important in life,* **Breakfast.**

Spot, *Refer:* **Thoughtful Spot.**

Spotted Backson, *Refer:* **Backson.**

Spreading, *adjective:* Crowding, in the wrong places, and all at once.

'Christopher Robin,' [Eeyore] said, 'we've come to say – to give you – it's called – written by – but we've all – because we've heard, I mean we all know – well, you see, it's – we – you – well, that, to put it as shortly as possible, is what it is.' He turned round angrily on the others and said, 'Everybody crowds round so in this Forest. There's no Space. I never saw a more Spreading lot of animals in my life, and all in the wrong places. Can't you *see* that Christopher Robin wants to be alone? I'm going.' And he humped off.

Not quite knowing why, the others began edging away.

(**THE HOUSE AT POOH CORNER, page** 168)

See Also: **Jostle.**

Spudge, *noun*: To put it as nicely as possible, the sort of bath sponge that a bachelor might have lying around the house just in case he might use it *again,* which is doubtful because the last **Bath*** was decidedly *wet,* and everything seemed to stay wet for a long time afterward.

So [Kanga] got cross with Owl and said that his house was a Disgrace, all damp and dirty, and it was quite time it did tumble down. Look at that horrid bunch of toadstools growing out of the floor there! So Owl looked down, a little surprised because he didn't know about this, and then gave a short sarcastic laugh, and explained that that was his sponge, and that if people didn't know a perfectly ordinary bath-sponge when they saw it, things were coming to a pretty pass. '*Well!*' said Kanga, and Roo fell in quickly, crying, 'I *must* see Owl's sponge!

Oh, there it is! Oh, Owl! Owl, it isn't a sponge, it's a spudge! Do you know what a spudge is, Owl? It's when your sponge gets all –' and Kanga said, 'Roo, dear!' very quickly, because that's *not* the way to talk to anybyody who can spell TUESDAY.
(**THE HOUSE AT POOH CORNER**, pages 152–53)

Refer: **Disgrace;** *and* **Washing Nonsense (Behind The Ears).**

Sqoze, *noun*: The name of whatever it is that happens to your nose under great pressure (usually applied by having things being *on* it).

> *But it doesn't seem fair*
> *To a Friendly Bear*
> *To stiffen him out with a basket-chair.*
> *And a sort of sqoze*
> *Which grows and grows*
> *Is not too nice for his poor old nose.*
> (**THE HOUSE AT POOH CORNER**, page 136)

See Also: **Squch.**

Squch, *noun*: The discomfort, similar to having a toothache, caused by a physical pressure on your neck, mouth, or ears, but not your nose (in which case the correct word is **Sqoze***).

> *And a sort of squch*
> *Is much too much*
> *For his neck and his mouth and his ears and such.*
> **(THE HOUSE AT POOH CORNER, page 136)**

Stornry, *adjective*: **1** *extraordinary,* which means, yes, it is very hard to believe that whatever it is that is claimed can be done is at all possible. **2** unbelievably good, or too good to be believable.

And as they went, Tigger told Roo (who wanted to know) all about the things that Tiggers could do.

'Can they fly?' asked Roo.

'Yes,' said Tigger, 'they're very good flyers, Tiggers are. Stornry good flyers.'

'Oo!' said Roo. 'Can they fly as well as Owl?'

'Yes,' said Tigger. 'Only they don't want to.'

'Why don't they want to?'

'Well, they just don't like it, somehow.'

Roo couldn't understand this, because he thought it would be lovely to be able to fly, but Tigger said it was difficult to explain to anybody who wasn't a Tigger himself.

(THE HOUSE AT POOH CORNER, pages 58–59)

Stoutness Exercises, *noun*: Calisthenics designed for the maintenance of a *certain* body shape, usually very rotund and cheerful.

[Pooh] had made up a little hum that very morning, as he was doing his Stoutness Exercises in front of the glass: *Tra-la-la, tra-la-la,* as he stretched up as high as he could go, and then *Tra-la-la, tra-la – oh, help! – la,* as he tried to reach his toes.

(WINNIE-THE-POOH, page 19)

See Also: **Bear, Eating Habits Thereof; Shortness of Breath;** *and* **Tra-La-La.**

Strange Animal, *phrasal noun:* **1** any animal that is unknown to us and, worse, doesn't act, behave, or do things like us. **2** any animal that doesn't know who 'us' is, and so must, by definition, not be one of us. **3** any animal so neat that it can carry all that it values in its pockets (unlike us).

'Here – we – are,' said Rabbit very slowly and carefully, 'all – of – us, and then, suddenly, we wake up one morning and, what do we find? We find a Strange Animal among us. An animal of whom we have never even heard before! An animal who carries her family about with her in her pocket! Suppose *I* carried *my* family about with me in *my* pocket, how many pockets should I want?'

'Sixteen,' said Piglet.

'Seventeen, isn't it?' said Rabbit. 'And one more for a handkerchief – that's eighteen. Eighteen pockets in one suit! I haven't time.'

There was a long and thoughtful silence . . . and then Pooh, who had been frowning very hard for some minutes, said: '*I* make it fifteen.'

(WINNIE-THE-POOH, pages 82–83)

Winnie-the-Pooh woke up suddenly in the middle of the night and listened . . . .

He got out of bed and opened his front door.

'Hallo!' said Pooh, in case there was anything outside.

'Hallo!' said Whatever-it-was.

'Oh!' said Pooh. 'Hallo!'

'Hallo!'

'Oh, *there* you are!' said Pooh. 'Hallo!'

'Hallo!' said the Strange Animal, wondering how long this was going on.

Pooh was just going to say 'Hallo!' for the fourth time when he thought that he wouldn't, so he said: 'Who is it?' instead.

'Me,' said a voice.

'Oh!' said Pooh. 'Well, come here.' . . . .

'Oh!' said Pooh, for he had never seen an animal like this before.

(THE HOUSE AT POOH CORNER, pages 18–20)

See Also: **Motherly;** *and* **Whatever-It-Was.**

Strengthening Medicine, *Refer:* Medicine.

Sudden and Temporary Immersion (the Important Thing to Do), *a safety tip*: Falling unawares into water is less harmful to your person if you keep your head out of the water. If you do this, then you are swimming. If not, it is very **Serious***.

> There came a sudden squeak from Roo, a splash, and a loud cry of alarm from Kanga.
>
> 'So much for *washing*,' said Eeyore.
>
> 'Roo's fallen in!' cried Rabbit, and he and Christopher Robin came rushing down to the rescue.
>
> 'Look at me swimming!' squeaked Roo from the middle of his pool, and was hurried down a waterfall into the next pool.

'Are you all right, Roo dear?' called Kanga anxiously.

'Yes!' said Roo. 'Look at me sw –' and down he went over the next waterfall into another pool.

Everybody was doing something to help. Piglet, wide awake suddenly, was jumping up and down and making 'Oo, I say' noises; Owl was explaining that in a case of Sudden and Temporary Immersion the Important Thing was to keep the Head Above Water; Kanga was jumping along the bank, saying 'Are you *sure* you're all right, Roo dear?' to which Roo, from whatever pool he was in at the moment, was answering 'Look at me swimming!'

(**WINNIE-THE-POOH, pages 111–12**)

See Also: **Bath; Rescue is Coming;** *and* **Washing Nonsense (Behind the Ears).**

Surprise, *Refer:* **Accident;** *and* **Ambush.**

Suspect, *verb:* To be aware of the obvious when others might not be.

Where should they dig the Very Deep Pit?

Piglet said that the best place would be somewhere where a Heffalump was, just before he fell into it, only about a foot farther on.

'But then he would see us digging it,' said Pooh.

'Not if he was looking at the sky.'

'He would Suspect,' said Pooh, 'if he happened to look down.' He thought for a long time and then added sadly, 'It isn't as easy as I thought. I suppose that's why Heffalumps hardly *ever* get caught.'

(WINNIE-THE-POOH, page 54)

Sustaining Book, *phrasal noun*: A book that encourages you during a time of hardship. (Note: The book cannot be eaten, although it is uncertain what other uses a book would have if you can't read.)

So [Pooh] started to climb out of the hole. He pulled with his front paws, and pushed with his back paws, and in a little while his nose was out in the open again . . . and then his ears . . . and then his front paws . . . and then his shoulders . . . and then –

'Oh, help!' said Pooh. 'I'd better go back.' . . .

'The fact is,' said Rabbit, 'you're stuck.'

'It all comes,' said Pooh crossly, 'of not having front doors big enough.'

'It all comes,' said Rabbit sternly, 'of cating too much . . . . '

'Then there's only one thing to be done,' [Christopher Robin] said. 'We shall have to wait for you to get thin again.'

'How long does getting thin take?' asked Pooh anxiously.

'About a week, I should think.' . . . .

'A week!' said Pooh gloomily. '*What about meals?*'

'I'm afraid no meals,' said Christopher Robin, 'because of getting thin quicker. But we *will* read to you.'

Bear began to sigh, and then found he couldn't because he was so tightly stuck; and a tear rolled down his eye, as he said:

'Then would you read a Sustaining Book, such as would help and comfort a Wedged Bear in Great Tightness?'

(WINNIE-THE-POOH, pages 23–26)

See Also: **Wedged in Great Tightness.**

Swimming Animals, *phrasal noun*: Those animals who manage to keep their heads above water while actually in the water.

But Tigger was holding on to the branch and saying to himself: . . . . 'It's quite different for Swimming Animals like Tiggers.' And he thought of himself floating on his back down a

river, or striking out from one island to another, and he felt that that was really the life for a Tigger.

(**THE HOUSE AT POOH CORNER, page 68**)

See Also: **Accident; Floating Bear; Sudden and Temporary Immersion (The Important Thing to Do,)** *and* **Umbrella.**

Tt

Tablecloth,
Refer: **Worraworraworraworraworra**.

Tail, *Refer:* **Little Bit Extra.**

Tea, *noun:* The activity of eating pleasant things in Friendly **Company***. There are several types:

    1. Very Nearly Tea (in which you don't need to use a plate but can eat straight from the biscuit jar);

2. Tea (exactly like Luncheon Time* but usually in the afternoon);

3. Proper Tea (napkins and washed faces required).

Christopher Robin was at home by this time, because it was the afternoon, and he was so glad to see them that they stayed there until very nearly tea-time, and then they had a Very Nearly tea, which is one you forget about afterwards, and hurried on to Pooh Corner, so as to see Eeyore before it was too late to have a Proper Tea with Owl.

(**THE HOUSE AT POOH CORNER**, page 128)

See Also: **Breakfast;** *and* **Eleven O'Clock**.

Terrible Flood, *Refer:* **Very Great Danger.**

Terrifying Journey, *Refer:* **Fly.**

That Accounts for a Good Deal, *Refer:* **It Explains Everything.**

Ther, *particle* (that is, what is called in Grammar a *particle,* which is a thing that looks like a word but does not act like a word. Particles are used in various ways, but one way is to attach a particle to a proper word and so change that word's meaning.

So, *ther* does this by making a girl's name into a boy's name, although it will still look like a girl's name but with *ther* attached to it. No one knows why this is so, which just proves it must be very good English to do it like that): *ther*.

When I first heard his name, I said, just as you are going to say, 'But I thought he was a boy?'

'So did I,' said Christopher Robin.

'Then you can't call him Winnie?'

'I don't.'

'But you said –'

'He's Winnie-ther-Pooh. Don't you know what '*ther*' means?'

'Ah, yes, now I do,' I said quickly; and I hope you do too, because it is all the explanation you are going to get.

(**WINNIE-THE-POOH**, pages 1–2)

Thingish, *adjective*: Like a *thing* as much as possible, or as near as you can imagine it.

Pooh began to feel a little more comfortable, because when you are a Bear of Very Little Brain, and you Think of Things, you find sometimes that a Thing which seemed very Thingish inside you is quite different when it gets out in the open and has other people looking at it.

(**THE HOUSE AT POOH CORNER**, page 99)

See Also: **Very Little Brain**.

Thing You Discover, *Refer*: **North Pole.**

Think, *Refer*: **Brain;** *and* **Fluff.**

Thinking Walk, *phrasal noun*: What you do on your own to get the **Fluff*** fluffing (or if you are lucky enough to have one, the **Brain*** braining), which can be quite annoying and bothersome if you had planned rather to sit with a friend and watch him doing things.

> One day when Pooh Bear had nothing else to do, he thought he would do something, so he went round to Piglet's house to see what Piglet was doing . . . . Piglet wasn't there.
>
> 'He's out,' said Pooh sadly. 'That's what it is. He's not in. I shall have to go a fast Thinking Walk by myself. Bother!'
>
> **(THE HOUSE AT POOH CORNER, page 1)**

See Also: **Short Walk.**

Thought for Others, *phrasal noun*: What is required to avoid using other people's **Food*** as seating.

> [Eeyore] looked round at them in his melancholy way. 'I suppose none of you are sitting on a thistle by any chance?'
>
> 'I believe I am,' said Pooh. 'Ow!' He got up, and looked behind him. 'Yes, I was. I thought so.'

'Thank you, Pooh. If you've quite finished with it.' He moved across to Pooh's place, and began to eat.

'It don't do them any Good, you know, sitting on them,' he went on, as he looked up munching. 'Takes all the Life out of them. Remember that another time, all of you. A little Consideration, a little Thought for Others, makes all the difference.'

(**WINNIE-THE-POOH, page 109**)

Thoughtful Spot, *phrasal noun*: That private place where friends can meet, usually, not to think at all but to talk, gossip, and wonder why they met at all (but in a dreamy, nice sort of a way).

Half way between Pooh's house and Piglet's house was a Thoughtful Spot where they met sometimes when they had decided to go and see each other, and as it was warm and out of the wind they would sit down there for a little and wonder what they would do now that they *had* seen each other. One day when they had decided not to do anything, Pooh made up a verse about it, so that everybody should know what the place was for.

This warm and sunny Spot
  Belongs to Pooh.
And here he wonders what
  He's going to do.
Oh, bother, I forgot –
  It's Piglet's too.

(THE HOUSE AT POOH CORNER, page 125)

See Also: **Company.**

Tiddely Pom, *onomatopoeic noun*: The real sound that snowflakes make hitting the ground, having fallen fifteen million feet.

The more it snows
  (Tiddely pom),
The more it goes
  (Tiddely pom),
The more it goes
  (Tiddely pom),
On snowing.

(THE HOUSE AT POOH CORNER, page 2)

Time-for-A-Little-Something, *phrasal noun*: **Eleven O'clock*** or close to it.

> And it was eleven o'clock.
> Which was Time-for-a-little-something.
> (**THE HOUSE AT POOH CORNER**, **page 55**)

Tole, *verb*: Purposeful misspelling of *told* for heightened poetic effect. *Refer:* **Pole.**

Too Late Now, *phrasal noun*: The moment which just a minute ago would have been the Right Time but isn't any more.

> As soon as Rabbit was out of sight, Pooh remembered that he had forgotten to ask who Small was, and whether he was the sort of friend-and-relation who settled on one's nose, or the sort who got trodden on by mistake, and as it was Too Late Now, he thought he would begin the Hunt by looking for Piglet, and asking him.
> (**THE HOUSE AT POOH CORNER**, **page 37**)

See Also: **Afterwards.**

Tracking Something, *Refer:* **Hunt.**

Tra-la-la, *meaningless noise*: **1** the hum to hum

when doing **Stoutness Exercises***. **2** hence, any hum that takes your mind off pain and tension.

See Also: **Remove Stiffness;** *and* **Shortness of Breath.**

Trap, *Refer:* **Cunning Trap; Heffalump Trap [for Poohs];** *and* **Very Deep Pit.**

Trespassers W, *noun:* The name of Piglet's house, *from* the name of his grandfather.

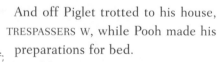

And off Piglet trotted to his house, TRESPASSERS W, while Pooh made his preparations for bed.

(WINNIE-THE-POOH, page 57)

See Also: **Grandfathers;** *and* **Trespassers William.**

Trespassers Will, *abbreviated name*: Short form of **Trespassers William***.

Trespassers William, *noun*: Any animal who needs two of everything, *from* the fact that Piglet had a grandfather who had two names because he was always losing them (as well as his Breath later on. *Refer:* **Shortness of Breath**).

Next to [Piglet's] house was a piece of broken board which had: 'TRESPASSERS W' on it. When Christopher Robin asked the Piglet what it meant, he said it was his grandfather's name, and had been in the family for a long time. Christopher Robin said you *couldn't* be called Trespassers W, and Piglet said yes, you could, because his grandfather was, and it was short for Trespassers Will, which was short for Trespassers William. And his grandfather had had two names in case he lost one – Trespassers after an uncle, and William after Trespassers.

'I've got two names,' said Christopher Robin carelessly.

'Well, there you are, that proves it,' said Piglet.

(**WINNIE-THE-POOH, pages 30–31**)

See Also: **Rabbit; Sanders;** *and* **Spelling.**

Twy-stymes, *noun:* **1** arithmetic if it has to do with the number two (**2**) (which is always a good number to have when doing anything). **2** multiplication table of the number two (**2**).

'In fact,' said Rabbit, coming to the end of it at last, 'Tigger's getting so Bouncy nowadays that it's time we taught him a lesson. Don't you think so, Piglet?' . . . .

The word 'lesson' came back to Pooh as one he had heard before somewhere.

'There's a thing called Twy-stymes,' he said. 'Christopher Robin tried to teach it to me once, but it didn't.'

'What didn't?' said Rabbit.

'Didn't what?' said Piglet.

Pooh shook his head.

'I don't know,' he said. 'It just didn't.'

(THE HOUSE AT POOH CORNER, pages 106, 108)

See Also: **Education; Instigorate;** *and* **Learn in Books.**

Uu

Umbrella, *noun*: A useful and adequate boat when necessary.

> 'We might go in your umbrella,' said Pooh.
> '!!!!!!'

For suddenly Christopher Robin saw that they might. He opened his umbrella and put it point downwards in the water. It floated but wobbled. Pooh got in. He was just beginning to say that it was all right now, when he found that it wasn't, so after a short drink which he didn't really want he waded back to Christopher Robin. Then they both got in together, and it wobbled no longer.

'I shall call this boat *The Brain of Pooh*,' said Christopher Robin, and *The Brain of Pooh* set sail forthwith in a south-westerly direction, revolving gracefully.

(WINNIE-THE-POOH, pages 130–31)

Compare: **Accident.**

Uncheer, *verb*: To be in a **Very Sad Condition*** and in desperate need of some fun and frivolity.

'I'm giving this to Eeyore,' [Pooh] explained, 'as a present. What are *you* going to give?'

'Couldn't I give it too?' said Piglet. 'From both of us?'

'No,' said Pooh. 'That would *not* be a good plan.'

'All right, then, I'll give him a balloon. I've got one left from my party. I'll go and get it now, shall I?'

'That, Piglet, is a *very* good idea. It is just what Eeyore wants to cheer him up. Nobody can be uncheered with a balloon.'

(WINNIE-THE-POOH, page 71)

Refer: **Balloon.**
See Also: **Friendly Day.**

Uncomfortable, *Refer:* **Foolish** *and* **Uncomfortable.**

Underneath, *noun*: That embarrassing condition of always being in a certain position when someone else decides also to be present in that position, which ends up with a disappointing exchange of weights and bruises. Similar to wrestling but less fun.

> 'Pooh!' squeaked the voice.
>
> 'It's Piglet!' cried Pooh eagerly. 'Where are you?'
>
> 'Underneath,' said Piglet in an underneath sort of way.
>
> 'Underneath what?'
>
> 'You,' squeaked Piglet. 'Get up!'
>
> 'Oh!' said Pooh, and scrambled up as quickly as he could. 'Did I fall on you, Piglet?'
>
> 'You fell on me,' said Piglet, feeling himself all over.
>
> 'I didn't mean to,' said Pooh sorrowfully.
>
> 'I didn't mean to be underneath,' said Piglet sadly.

(THE HOUSE AT POOH CORNER, pages 40–41)

See Also: **Accident;** *and* **Very Good Dropper.**

Under the Name, *Refer:* **Sanders.**

Unsettle, *verb*: To purposely *or* accidentally confuse Smaller Animals by talking in funny voices and looking at them fiercely.

'Ho-*ho*!' said Christopher Robin loudly and suddenly . . . .

'It's the Heffalump!' thought Piglet nervously. 'Now, then!' He hummed in his throat a little, so that none of the words should stick, and then, in the most delightfully easy way, he said: 'Tra-la-la, tra-la-la,' as if he had just thought of it. But he didn't look round, because if you look round and see a Very Fierce Heffalump looking down at you, sometimes you forget what you were going to say.

'Rum-tum-tum-tiddle-um,' said Christopher Robin in a voice like Pooh's . . . .

'How *did* you get there, Piglet?' said Christopher Robin in his ordinary voice.

'This is Terrible,' thought Piglet. 'First he talks in Pooh's voice, and then he talks in Christopher Robin's voice, and he's doing it so as to Unsettle me.' And being now Completely Unsettled, he said very quickly and squeakily: 'This is a trap for Poohs, and I'm waiting to fall in it, ho-*ho*, what's all this, and then I say ho-*ho* again.'

'*What*?' said Christopher Robin.

'A trap for ho-ho's,' said Piglet huskily. 'I've just made it, and I'm waiting for the ho-ho to come-come.'

(THE HOUSE AT POOH CORNER, pages 47–49)

220

See Also: **Pluck;** *and* **Rabbit.**

Upsetting Heffalumps, *Refer:* Ho-Ho!

Upstairs Going, *Refer:* Bumping.

Useful, *adjective*: Having the right qualities (smallness, roundness, and braveness) to do what has to be done, especially if you're a Very Small Animal.

> 'It is hard to be brave,' said Piglet, sniffing slightly, 'when you're only a Very Small Animal.'
> Rabbit, who had begun to write very busily, looked up and said:
> 'It is because you are a very small animal that you will be Useful in the adventure before us.'
> Piglet was so excited at the idea of being Useful that he forgot to be frightened any more, and . . . he was so eager to begin being useful at once.

(**Winnie-the-Pooh,** pages 84–85)

See Also: **Blinch; Pluck;** *and* **Size, Favourite.**

Usual Way, *phrasal noun*: If one doesn't know what this means, one cannot be told.

Nobody seemed to know where they came from, but there they were in the Forest: Kanga and Baby Roo. When Pooh asked Christopher Robin, 'How did they come here?' Christopher Robin said, 'In the Usual Way, if you know what I mean, Pooh,' and Pooh, who didn't, said 'Oh!' Then he nodded his head twice and said, 'In the Usual Way. Ah!' Then he went to call upon his friend Piglet to see what *he* thought about it.

(**Winnie-the-Pooh**, page 81)

Very Bad Accident, *useful phrase*: It is often useful to say this during, or immediately following, an **Accident*** to see how **Serious*** it all is. If you can't say it, or some other words come out, *get help*!

> 'There you are! I say things when I'm not trying. So it must be a very bad Accident.' And then he thought that perhaps when he did try to say things he wouldn't be able to; so, to make sure, he said loudly: 'A Very Bad Accident to Pooh Bear.'

(THE HOUSE AT POOH CORNER, pages 39–40)

Very Clever Brain, *phrasal noun*: The sort of mind that can devise **Cunning Traps*** to capture Larger Animals, although what you do **Afterwards*** remains Uncertain.

They sighed and got up; and when they had taken a few gorse prickles out of themselves they sat down again; and all the time Pooh was saying to himself, 'If only I could *think* of something!' For he felt sure that a Very Clever Brain could catch a Heffalump if only he knew the right way to go about it.

(**WINNIE-THE-POOH, page 54**)

Refer: **Very Deep Pit.**
Compare: **Brain.**

Very Clever Pup-Pup-Pup Plan,

phrasal noun: Any plan that is quite clever, but involves **Anxiety*** and Fortitude (in unequal amounts), if not Danger to Your Person.

Refer: **Very Grand Thing.**

Very Deep Pit, *phrasal noun*: A hole dug in the ground of such depth that even a Fierce Heffalump couldn't climb out of it (should it, by any chance, actually be persuaded to climb into the hole or should it even fall into the hole, for that matter).

'I have decided to catch a Heffalump.' Pooh nodded his head several times as he said this, and waited for Piglet to say 'How?' or 'Pooh, you couldn't!' or something helpful of that sort, but Piglet said nothing. The fact was Piglet was wishing that *he* had thought about it first.

'I shall do it,' said Pooh, after waiting a little longer, 'by means of a trap. And it must be a Cunning Trap, so you will have to help me, Piglet.' . . . .

Pooh's first idea was that they should dig a Very Deep Pit, and then the Heffalump . . . might be walking along, humming a little song, and looking up at the sky, wondering if it would rain, and so he wouldn't see the Very Deep Pit until he was half-way down, when it would be too late.

Piglet said that this was a very good Trap, but supposing it were raining already?

Pooh rubbed his nose again, and said that he hadn't thought of that. And then he brightened up, and said that, if it were raining already, the

Heffalump would be looking at the sky wondering if it would *clear up,* and so he wouldn't see the Very Deep Pit until he was half-way down . . . When it would be too late.

Piglet said that, now that this point had been explained, he thought it was a Cunning Trap.

Pooh was very proud when he heard this, and he felt that the Heffalump was as good as caught already.

(WINNIE-THE-POOH, pages 52–54)

See Also: **Heffalump Trap (for Poohs).**

Very Good Dropper, *phrasal noun*: Any animal that is able not only to climb a tree but also to fall out of one without hurting itself. Usually, however, a Very Good Dropper doesn't get hurt because it has someone to fall *upon* (as this always softens the landing).

'Look, Pooh!' said Piglet suddenly. 'There's something in one of the Pine Trees.'

'So there is!' said Pooh, looking up wonderingly. 'There's an Animal.'

Piglet took Pooh's arm, in case Pooh was frightened.

'Is it One of the Fiercer Animals?' he said, looking the other way.

Pooh nodded.

'It's a Jagular,' he said.

'What do Jagulars do?' asked Piglet, hoping that they wouldn't.

'They hide in the branches of trees, and drop on you as you go underneath,' said Pooh. 'Christopher Robin told me.'

'Perhaps we better hadn't go underneath, Pooh. In case he dropped and hurt himself.'

'They don't hurt themselves,' said Pooh. 'They're such very good droppers.'

Piglet still felt that to be underneath a Very Good Dropper would be a Mistake, and he was just going to hurry back for something which he had forgotten when the Jagular called out to them.

'Help! Help!' it called.

'That's what Jagulars always do,' said Pooh, much interested. 'They call "Help! Help!" and then when you look up, they drop on you.'

'I'm looking *down*,' cried Piglet loudly, so as the Jagular shouldn't do the wrong thing by accident.

(THE HOUSE AT POOH CORNER, pages 62–64)

See Also: **Underneath.**

Very Good Idea, *phrasal noun*: Any Idea that might actually lead to stopping a very unpleasant habit in a very active Larger Animal (*larger* in the sense of at least being *bigger* than you are).

Piglet said that Tigger *was* very Bouncy, and that if they could think of a way of unbouncing him, it would be a Very Good Idea.
(**THE HOUSE AT POOH CORNER, page 107**)
See Also: **Grand Idea.**

Very Grand Thing, *phrasal noun*: When a Very Small Animal overcomes its Uncertainty and does the Right Thing.

This was not very comforting to Piglet, because however many pieces of string they tried pulling up with, it would always be the same him coming down; but still, it did seem the only thing to do. So with one last look back in his mind at all the happy hours he had spent in the Forest *not* being pulled up to the ceiling by a piece of string, Piglet nodded bravely at Pooh and said that it was a Very Clever pup-pup-pup Clever pup-pup Plan.

'It won't break,' whispered Pooh comfortingly, 'because you're a Small Animal,

228

and I'll stand underneath, and if you save us all, it will be a Very Grand Thing to talk about afterwards.'

(THE HOUSE AT POOH CORNER, page 139)

See Also: **Respectful Song.**

Very Great Danger, *phrasal noun:* A threat to you that is imagined rather than real, although the long wait for rescue could be highly dangerous.

You can imagine Piglet's joy when at last the ship came in sight of him. In after-years he liked to think that he had been in Very Great Danger during the Terrible Flood, but the only danger he had really been in was the last half-hour of his imprisonment, when Owl, who had just flown up, sat on a branch of his tree to comfort him, and told him a very long story about an aunt who had once laid a seagull's egg by mistake, and the story went on and on, rather like this sentence, until Piglet who was listening out of his window without much hope, went to sleep quietly and naturally, slipping slowly out of the window towards the water until he was only hanging on by his toes, at which moment luckily, a sudden loud squawk from Owl, which was really part of the story, being what his aunt said, woke the Piglet up and just gave him time to jerk himself back into safety and say, 'How interesting, and did she?'

(WINNIE-THE-POOH, pages 131–32)

See Also: **Interesting Anecdote.**

Very Happy Birthday, *Refer:* Hipy Papy Bthuthdth Thuthda Bthuthdy.

Very Happy Thursday, *phrasal noun:* The excuse to give if you and your friends want to get together in **Company*** (with **Smackerels*** and Hilarity), perhaps only because it seems a **Friendly Day*,** and it doesn't seem necessary to wait for a Proper Occasion to Celebrate.

> Piglet thought that they ought to have a Reason for going to see everybody . . . if Pooh could think of something.
> Pooh could.
> 'We'll go because it's Thursday,' he said, 'and we'll go to wish everybody a Very Happy Thursday. Come on, Piglet.'

(THE HOUSE AT POOH CORNER, page 126)

Compare: **Important Thing.**

Very Important Missage, *Refer:* Missage.

Very Little Brain, *phrasal noun*: What Smallish – well, Stoutish – Animals have that makes them feel or sense things that ordinary everyday words couldn't describe. So, these Smallish (well, Stoutish) Animals feel **Singy*** and do **Hums***. It is a gift, if you are a poet, to see and know things that other people are too busy to notice.

'That it isn't,' said Pooh.
'Isn't what?'
Pooh knew what he meant, but, being a Bear of Very Little Brain, couldn't think of the words.
'Well, it just isn't,' he said again.
(THE HOUSE AT POOH CORNER, page 43)

Refer: **Positively Startling Lack of Brain.**

Very Nearly Tea, *Refer*: **Tea.**

Very Sad Condition, *phrasal noun*: A state of rejection, usually triggered by the complete indifference shown by everyone else to your existence.

'Hallo, Pooh,' said Piglet.
'What are *you* trying to do?'
'I was trying to reach the knocker,' said Piglet. 'I just came round –'

'Let me do it for you,' said Pooh kindly. So he reached up and knocked at the door. 'I have just seen Eeyore,' he began, 'and poor Eeyore is in a Very Sad Condition, because it's his birthday, and nobody has taken any notice of it, and he's very Gloomy – you know what Eeyore is – and there he was, and – What a long time whoever lives here is answering this door.' And he knocked again.

'But Pooh,' said Piglet, 'it's your own house!'

'Oh!' said Pooh. 'So it is,' he said. 'Well, let's go in.'

(WINNIE-THE-POOH, pages 70–71)

See Also: **Gloomy; How;** *and* **Inasmuch as Which.**

Ww

Waiting to Catch Up, *same as*: HUNT.

Washing Nonsense (Behind the Ears), *donkey theory*: **1** the criticism of a modern trend toward making everyone, sooner or later, not only clean *behind the ears* (that area found on your head that is not quite the back of your ears and not quite the back of your head) but the face as well, and even take full **Baths***. **2** generally, a criticism of any trend or belief that holds that any Animal, Smaller or Larger, and whatever its Disposition, or Size, or Shape, or Circumstance, would be a better Animal by changing its worn-in and comfortable color, as if Dignity and **Respect*** are only soap deep.

Piglet was lying on his back, sleeping peacefully. Roo was washing his face and paws in the stream, while Kanga explained to everybody proudly that this was the first time he had ever washed his face himself . . .

'I don't hold with all this washing,' grumbled Eeyore. 'This modern Behind-the-ears nonsense. What do *you* think, Pooh?'

'Well,' said Pooh, '*I* think –' . . . .

There came a sudden squeak from Roo, a splash, and a loud cry of alarm from Kanga.

'So much for *washing*,' said Eeyore.

(WINNIE-THE-POOH, pages 110–11)

Wedged in Great Tightness, *descriptive phrase*: What you are when Plump and Poorly Positioned in an Undersized Space.

Refer: **Sustaining Book.**

West Pole (yet another Pole that lies undiscovered). *Refer*: **East Pole; North Pole;** *and* **Poles (Other).**

Whatever-It-Was, *phrasal noun*: Exactly like a **Strange Animal*,** but without a name.

What-nots, *noun*: Those animals in a Poetry audience who have no literary appreciation.

234

Refer: **Etceteras.**

What-Shall-I-Do-About-You-Know-What, *phrasal noun*: A heart-to-heart talk on an interesting or diverting problem.

'Come on, Pooh,' [said Christopher Robin] and walked off quickly.

'Where are we going?' said Pooh, hurrying after him, and wondering whether it was to be an Explore or a What-shall-I-do-about-you-know-what.

'Nowhere,' said Christopher Robin.

So they began going there.

(**THE HOUSE AT POOH CORNER, page 168**)

See Also: **Company; Nothing;** *and* **Thoughtful Spot.**

Compare: **Seeing What Everybody Else Thought About It.**

Winnie-the-Pooh, *Refer:* **Edward Bear; Sanders; Sir Pooh De Bear, Knight; Ther;** *and* **Winnie-The-Pooh, Honorific Titles Thereof.**

Winnie-the-Pooh, Honorific Titles Thereof, many and various, including:

> **E.C. AND T.F.***
> **Edward Bear***
> **Eeyore's Comforter and Tail-finder***
> **F.O.P.***
> **Friend of Piglet's***
> **P.D.***
> **Pooh**
> **PooH***
> **Pole Discoverer***
> **Rabbit's Companion***
> **R.C.***
> **Sanders***
> **Sir Pooh de Bear, Knight***

And then this Bear, Pooh Bear, Winnie-the-Pooh, F.O.P. (Friend of Piglet's), R.C. (Rabbit's Companion), P.D. (Pole Discoverer), E.C. and T.F. (Eeyore's Comforter and Tail-finder) – in fact, Pooh himself.

(WINNIE-THE-POOH, page 129)

Wizzle, *noun*: **1** a Fierce Animal of unknown Appearance and Temperament (not as common as the **Woozle***). **2** hence, any Animal of unknown Temperament (but assumed to be Fierce).

'*What?*' said Piglet, with a jump. And then, to show that he hadn't been frightened, he jumped up and down once or twice in an exercising sort of way.

'The tracks!' said Pooh. '*A third animal has joined the other two!*'

'Pooh!' cried Piglet. 'Do you think it is another Woozle?'

'No,' said Pooh, 'because it makes different

marks. It is either Two Woozles and one, as it might be, Wizzle, or Two, as it might be, Wizzles and one, if so it is, Woozle. Let us continue to follow them.'

So they went on, feeling a little anxious now.

(**WINNIE-THE-POOH, pages 34–35**)

See Also: **Fierce Animal;** *and* **Hostile Intent.**

Wobble, *verb*: The way certain letters and words deliberately cause difficulties and problems, so that, no matter how you might try, you can't do **Spelling*.**

[Owl said,] 'You ought to write "*A Happy Birthday*" on it.'

'*That* was what I wanted to ask you,' said Pooh. 'Because my spelling is Wobbly. It's good spelling but it Wobbles, and the letters get in the wrong places. Would *you* write "A Happy Birthday" on it for me?' . . . .

Well, he washed the pot out, and dried it, while Owl licked the end of his pencil, and wondered how to spell 'birthday.'

'Can you read, Pooh?' he asked, a little anxiously.

(**WINNIE-THE-POOH, pages 73–74**)

See Also: **A.**

Woozle, *noun*: An Unfriendly Animal to most animals except **Wizzles*** (with whom they share a passion for the outdoors, going around in pairs or small groups for long winter walks). *Refer*: **Wizzle.**

Worraworraworraworraworra, *loud exclamation if not interjection*: The Terrible and Fearsome Battle Cry of an Unfierce Animal when entering into a fray with an even less Unfierce Animal (or, more usually, **Tablecloth***).

> Tigger said: 'Excuse me a moment, but there's something climbing up your table,' and with one loud *Worraworraworraworra* he jumped at the end of the tablecloth, pulled it to the ground, wrapped himself up in it three times, rolled to the other end of the room, and, after a terrible struggle, got his head into the daylight again, and said cheerfully: 'Have I won?'
>
> 'That's my tablecloth,' said Pooh, as he began to unwind Tigger.

> 'I wondered what it was,' said Tigger.
>
> 'It goes on the table and you put things on it.'
>
> 'Then why did it try to bite me when I wasn't looking?'

'I don't *think* it did,' said Pooh.

'It tried,' said Tigger, 'but I was too quick for it.'

(THE HOUSE AT POOH CORNER, pages 21–22)

See Also: **Fiercer Animal;** *and* **Strange Animal.**

Writing a Notice, *Refer:* Seeing What Every-Body Else Thought About It.

Wuss, *adjective:* Poetic form of *worse*. There is probably a very correct and literary word to describe what it is, but all it does is change the sound of a word so it rhymes better. And it is still the same word; it just *sings* a little differently.

> *For lo! the wind was blusterous*
> > *And flattened out his favourite tree;*
> > *And things looks bad for him and we –*
> *Looked bad, I mean, for he and us –*
> *I've never known them wuss.*

(from *Here lies a tree*)
(THE HOUSE AT POOH CORNER, page 145)

Xx

X, *noun*: One of the last letters in the alphabet (indeed, some say it is *the* last letter of the alphabet). Either **X** is Retiring and Slow, or perhaps, and just perhaps, **X** is one of those letters that forced poor **A** to go first. Isn't it true that **X** hardly ever goes first? In that case, **X** may very well have teeth (which comes as a Surprise now to Piglet, who is sure Pooh said once that it had a neck and not teeth).

'Oh! Piglet,' said Pooh excitedly, 'we're going on an Expotition, all of us, with things to eat. To discover something.'

'To discover what?' said Piglet anxiously.

'Oh! just something.'

'Nothing fierce?'

'Christopher Robin didn't say anything about fierce. He just said it had an "x".'

'It isn't their necks I mind,' said Piglet earnestly. 'It's their teeth. But if Christopher Robin is coming I don't mind anything.'

(**WINNIE-THE-POOH, pages 103–04**)

Yy

You Know What, *euphemism*: What you say to avoid embarrassing a Very Small Animal who is both very proud but deeply modest about having done a **Very Grand Thing***.

'Piglet,' said Pooh a little shyly, after they had walked for some time without saying anything.

'Yes, Pooh?'

'Do you remember when I said that a Respectful Pooh Song might be written about You Know What?'

'Did you, Pooh?' said Piglet, getting a little pink round the nose. 'Oh, yes, I believe you did.'

'It's been written, Piglet.'

The pink went slowly up Piglet's nose to his ears, and settled there.

(THE HOUSE AT POOH CORNER, pages 148–49)

See Also: **Blinch; Pluck;** *and* **Respectful Song.**

You know Why, *another euphemism*: What you say to avoid the embarrassment of telling anyone you may only have **Fluff*** after all (although everyone knows you do – have Fluff – but sometimes it's better not to make too big an issue of it).

> 'Hallo, Pooh,' said Rabbit.
>
> 'Hallo, Rabbit,' said Pooh dreamily.
>
> 'Did you make that song up?'
>
> 'Well, I sort of made it up,' said Pooh. 'It isn't Brain,' he went on humbly, 'because You Know Why, Rabbit; but it comes to me sometimes.'
>
> 'Ah!' said Rabbit, who never let things come to him, but always went and fetched them.
>
> **(THE HOUSE AT POOH CORNER, page 80)**

See Also: **Brain;** *and* **Positively Startling Lack of Brain.**

244

Zoo, *noun*: Where some Bears live.

When Christopher Robin goes to the Zoo, he goes to where the Polar Bears are, and he whispers something to the third keeper from the left, and doors are unlocked, and we wander through dark passages and up steep stairs, until at last we come to the special cage, and the cage is opened, and out trots something brown and furry, and with a happy cry of 'Oh, Bear!' Christopher Robin rushes into its arms. Now this bear's name is Winnie, which shows what a good

name for bears it is, but the funny thing is that
we can't remember whether Winnie is called
after Pooh, or Pooh after Winnie. We did know
once, but we have forgotten . . . .

(WINNIE-THE-POOH, Introduction)